The Fruitful Vine

A Celebration of Biblical Womanhood

Warren Henderson

THE FRUITFULL VINE
By Warren Henderson
Copyright © 2005

Published by GOSPEL FOLIO PRESS
304 Killaly Street West
Port Colborne, ON, L3K 6A6, Canada

ISBN 189-711-7132

Cover design by Daveen Lidstone & Rachel Brooks

All Scripture quotations from the King James
Version of the Bible unless otherwise noted.

Ordering Information:
GOSPEL FOLIO PRESS
1-905-835-9166
orders@gospelfolio.com
www.gospelfolio.com

Printed in the United States of America

Table of Contents

Table of Contents (Cont.)

Acknowledgements

The author is indebted to those who sacrificed time and talents to aid the publishing of *The Fruitful Vine*. I thank the Lord for each of the following and their contributions: Daveen Lidstone for cover design and layout. David Dunlap and Mike Attwood for technical editing. Caroline Cairns and Jane Biberstein for general editing. Annette Hanson, David Lindstrom, Gina Mulligan, and my dear wife Brenda for proofreading assistance.

Preface

"In the beginning God created the heaven and the earth," and for an encore, He created woman. God formed man from the dust of the earth, breathed an eternal spirit into him, and then drew woman from his side. As God's representative on earth, man was a spectacular crown to creation (Heb. 2:7). Then came woman, who was also a crown—a crown of honour to her husband (Prov. 12:4)—she was the crown of the crown. This superb allegory emphasizes the importance God ascribes to biblical womanhood as it relates to marriage. Unfortunately, this feminine ministry is greatly undervalued and generally misunderstood by modern society.

The whole of Scripture upholds marriage as God's general rule for humanity. Yet, it is understood that many Christian women are presently single. Many desire to be married, but God has yet to provide a husband for them. Some were once married but are now widows; others have been deserted. Other sisters have resolved to remain single to better serve the Lord Jesus in ministry. Such ministry is often transparent to the public eye, but in the spiritual realm, it has the praise of God and an eternal weight of glory. This book provides some encouragement for all my sisters, but plainly, the main focus is the woman's natural ministry for which she was created. It is recognized that there are alternate sacrificial callings and sovereign determinations beyond the general—to these we simply bow in reverence. Women who remain single can pursue serving the Lord without being hindered by marital and maternal duties (1 Cor. 7:34). Though singleness is not the natural purpose for the woman (or there would be few people indeed), the sister dedicated to serving in singleness is greatly appreciated and respected for her selfless love for the Lord Jesus!

It has been said that "an ideal wife is any woman who has an ideal husband" and "a good husband makes a good wife." Just as woman was fashioned from and for man, biblical manhood advocates biblical womanhood. For a wife to achieve full femininity, she must comprehend the divine purpose for which she was created, her husband must be satisfying her essential needs, and she must be sustained by God's grace for the strenuous responsibility. To this extent, this book is as much for men as it is for women. In the visible realm, few exhibitions of divine order can rival the loveliness of a wife settled in her calling and endeavouring to please her Creator through the pursuit of biblical womanhood. Perhaps the splendour of this sight is only comparable with the man who so identifies with Christ that his guidance and love for his wife is selfless and tenacious.

This book is divided into six sections. The first section, *The Marital Union*, supplies the biblical foundation for the remainder of the book: Why was marriage instituted, and what was God's best plan for marriage? The following three sections pertain to the main natural roles a married woman will find the most joy in fulfilling—namely, being a companion to her husband, bearing and nurturing children, and keeping an ordered home. The fifth section, *The Autumn Years*, provides counsel to the "empty-nesters" and encouragement for widows. The final section provides a character sketch of a spiritually-minded woman and the types of ministry she may engage in. God reveals both what He finds beautiful in a woman and what He expects her to do to please Him.

The Old Testament often applies the "vine" metaphor to the nation of Israel, but the vine is also employed to poetically speak of the blessings of a virtuous wife. We will explore and decipher each depiction of the vine as related to biblical wifehood, then apply the teaching through sensible helps for both men and women. Only when a wife appreciates and apprehends true femininity will she truly enjoy being a woman.

The Marital Union

The First Marriage

"And the Lord God said, It is not good that the man should be alone; I will make him an help meet (helper fit) for him" (Gen. 2:18). God observed Adam's loneliness and, with fathomless wisdom, created the finest solution—woman. It would cost Adam a rib, but the sacrifice would be a reminder that he and the woman were now one flesh and that he would only find completeness with her at his side.

The English word "rib" (found in Genesis 2:22) is not the best translation of the Hebrew word *tsela*. *Tsela* appears forty-four times in the Old Testament and is translated only here as "rib"; most commonly, it is translated "side." God took part of Adam's side to create woman and then closed up the remaining flesh. In the "operation," God took flesh, bone and blood, for *"the life of the flesh is in the blood"* (Lev. 17:11). Adam's first words to his wife confirm that more than a rib was taken: *"This is now bone of my bones, and flesh of my flesh; she shall be called Woman, because she was taken out of Man"* (Gen. 2:23). Woman was created to be her husband's companion and helper and to remain at his side from where she was extracted. She was drawn from under her husband's arm, and there, too, she would find comfort and protection.

The woman was to be man's companion, friend, and helper. Praise God that Adam didn't ask for a teddy bear, or some other flawed substitute, for the only creation that would meet his need for companionship and resolve his aloneness was woman. Woman was designed not only to be man's helper and partner for life, but so that she, too, would find significance and security in the companionship of the man. In His divine wisdom, God created woman to satisfy Adam's need for companionship, but in creating the perfect partner for Adam, He also was planning the perfect mate for woman.

Everything that the woman became (spirit, soul, and body) was derived from Adam. When his companion was presented to him, he uttered *Isha*, or "woman," meaning "derived from man." Eve was as much a descendant of Adam as you and I are. By human procreation, everything that we are is derived from the dust of the earth and the original breath of God into Adam. Adam was created as an innocent living soul, but became degraded by personal sin. We, in him, are also depraved (Rom. 5:12). Depravity is hereditary and requires regeneration by the Holy Spirit to resolve. Satan initially tempted the woman to eat the forbidden fruit, but the ultimate target was Adam, as recorded in Genesis 3. Eve, however, as a descendant of Adam, was not responsible for the human race. Her sin brought death to her, but to her only; whereas, Adam's sin ushered in death to all who would be derived from him.

Prior to the surgical procedure, Adam had likely seen most, if not all, of the animals because of his task of naming them. How insignificant everything on earth must have seemed after one glimpse of his new helper! The experience for the woman was different: When she opened her eyes for the first time, she saw the Lord, for God brought her to Adam. She knew nothing of her new world before meeting her companion, which allowed Adam to show his wife God's handiwork and to have the opportunity to appreciate it with her. Man has escorted woman ever since. Life's special moments are more exceptional when we have someone to share them with!

Man did not invent matrimony. God instituted marriage between one man and one woman in the beginning of human existence; thus, only His rules apply for marriage. Homosexuality is an abomination to the Lord and is nothing less than rebellion against His order (Lev. 18:22; 20:13; Rom. 1:24–32). Polygamy was never approved of by God (Deut. 17:17). Through the marriage covenant, God intended one man and one woman to become one person; this union would protect and sanctify every part of their relationship.

In the same way, the Church finds her significance and security in Christ even as the woman found her beginning, purpose, and dignity in Adam. It only cost Adam his side for his bride, but the price of Christ's bride was much higher—it cost Him His life. Yet, both the first Adam and the last Adam (Christ) were pleased with what their personal sacrifices obtained for them, the former a woman and the latter a multitude of redeemed souls (Isa. 53:11). Both the first marriage of the Bible and the last marriage of the Bible convey God's design for the integrity and permanence of the union. Henry Morris writes on this subject:

> It is true, of course, that with marriage as well as with all other human activities, *"God hath made man upright; but they have sought out many inventions" (Eccl. 7:29).* Polygamy, concubinage, polyandry, easy divorce, adultery, promiscuity, and other distortions of the marriage covenant have permeated many cultures; but, as the Lord Jesus said: *"From the beginning it was not so" (Matt. 19:8).*[1]

This one-person union is God's plan for every man and woman entering into a marriage covenant. *Therefore shall a man leave his father and his mother, and shall cleave unto his wife: and they shall be one flesh" (Gen. 2:24).* In the beginning, God stated that this was His best for humankind, and later, the

Lord Jesus confirmed that nothing had changed (Matt. 19:5-6). Through marriage, one man and one woman become *one flesh*. *One flesh* is a singular noun meaning one person. Concerning this relationship, Scripture refers to *"them,"* but also acknowledges *"he"* and *"she."* A husband and wife, though two different individuals, can no longer act independently. They cannot consider their own interests first; they must think and act as one person, which necessitates developing joint interests and engaging in activities together.

> One flesh is pictured by two pieces of paper glued together after the glue has dried. When they are pulled apart, pieces of both sheets still stick to each other.
>
> —Walter Trobisch

This oneness reality in marriage is at the heart of Paul's exhortation: *"So ought men to love their wives as their own bodies. He that loveth his wife loveth himself. For no man ever yet hated his own flesh, but nourisheth and cherisheth it, even as the Lord the church" (Eph. 5:28-29).* When a man sacrificially loves his wife, as he is commanded to do four times in Scripture (Eph. 5:25, 28, 33; Col. 3:19), his initiating love will naturally return to him. Wives love to love, but as designed and created, they require their husband's love to fully loosen their own love.

It is noted that a sexual relationship between a man and woman does not constitute a marriage covenant, although it consummates the covenant. Even in ancient days, an agreement was made between the families, and usually, a dowry was paid to the bride's father. If parental authority had been removed, a monarch oversaw the matter of arranging marriages. The Lord Jesus acknowledged that the man and the woman living together in John 4 were not married. In 1 Corinthians 6:16, Paul states that a man becomes one flesh with a harlot through an erotic relationship, but they are not married, for the reproof is to repent of this behaviour—not to marry the harlot. Exodus 22:16-17, Deuteronomy 22:13-21, and Genesis 34:4 all reference the fact that an unmarried virgin woman was not considered married after having been with a man. The marriage covenant sanctifies and protects the sexual union of a man and a woman, but this union outside marriage is just plain sin. Let us call it what it is.

God desired a deep sense of oneness to develop from the elaborate intertwining of two companions who would freely and openly mingle in every aspect. After Adam and his wife sinned, the harmonious oneness that they had enjoyed was spoiled. New individuality gripped their marriage, and feelings of guilt prompted withdrawal and isolation tendencies. Their sin not only made them uncomfortable with God, for they hid from His presence under trees of Eden, but also with each other, for now they knew that they were naked. Before sinning, not even clothes separated them, but after their rebellion, they sought to cover up and limit self-disclosure. This exemplifies the nature of human sin—it seeks what we are not and hides the reality of what we are. Only through Christ and the indwelling Spirit of God can such damage be repaired and a real sense of unity be developed in the marriage relationship again. With Christ at the helm, no reason exists for love deprivation within the Christian marriage or family.

The oneness that the man and woman initially shared is evident for God called *"Adam"* to arouse both hiding sinners from their reclusion. Genesis 5:2 reads, *"male and female created He them; and blessed them, and called **their name Adam**, in the day when they were created."* The man was created first and named Adam. When the woman was created from Adam, she

11

received no name except "woman," speaking of her origin—
"from man." She needed no personal name for she already had
one in Adam. Therefore, the garden experience of the woman in
relationship to the man may be summarized as follows: She was
made *for* Adam *from* Adam, *brought to* Adam, *led* Adam into
sin (1 Tim. 2:13-15), then ultimately was *named by* Adam after
their fall, which demonstrated his authority over her.

God upholds the equality of men and women throughout
Scripture (1 Cor. 11:11; Gal. 3:28). As Matthew Henry comments, even the creation of the woman was done to illustrate
both equality of the genders and the role of the husband towards his wife.

> The woman was made of a rib out of the side of Adam; not
> made out of his head to rule over him, nor out of his feet to
> be trampled upon by him, but out of his side to be equal with
> him, under his arm to be protected, and near his heart to be
> beloved.[2]

Until the fall of humankind, the peacefulness of God-
ordered headship governed family life in the garden. Satan's
temptation brought disorder and chaos into a perfect marital
relationship. After sin intruded into the first marriage and
caused disorder, God responded by reaffirming headship in the
marriage relationship to reestablish proper order. However, the
yearnings of self and the lusts of fallen flesh would forever rival the order God prescribed for marital bliss.

The spiritual resources of love, grace, and longsuffering are
available for every believer to draw upon in repairing the inherent damage that two people with sin natures will cause to any
marriage. Ephesians 1:3 reads, *"Blessed be the God and Father
of our Lord Jesus Christ, who hath blessed us with all spiritual
blessings in heavenly places in Christ."* Marriages need Christ

to mend the damage of sin and to nurture and equip mates to love each other unselfishly in order to survive and thrive in today's immoral, self-seeking culture. Only when both parties are pursuing Christ and experiencing His pure love will marital harmony be maintained.

"There seems to be friction in our home," a concerned wife said to a marriage counsellor. "I really don't know what the trouble is." "Friction is caused by one of two things," said the counsellor, and to illustrate he picked up two blocks of wood from his desk. "If one block is moving and one is standing still, there's friction. Or, if both are moving but in opposite directions, there's friction. Now, which is it?" "I'll have to admit that I've been going backward in my Christian life, and Joe has really been growing," the wife admitted. "What I need is to get back to fellowship with the Lord."[3] For the marriage experience to be joyful and fruitful, it must be centred in the Lord Jesus.

Certainly Philip Bliss, the prolific hymn writer, found this to be true in his marital relationship with his wife Lucy. William Guest, in his book *P. P. Bliss Songwriter*, highlights the fruitfulness of Philip and Lucy Bliss' joyful marriage despite hardships and disappointments. He also notes Philip's deep appreciation for his helper and companion:

In his diary he [Philip Bliss] wrote: "June 1st, 1859. Married to Miss Lucy J. Young; the very best thing I could have done." He never, in his deep thankfulness, kept back how much he owed to her. One sentence, written in 1874, is repeated in various forms all through those years—"We are well, happy, cheerful, and content." Health and sickness, joy and sorrow, were theirs; but he always found a moral support in the wife of his youth. At sixteen years of age she had avowed her love to Christ, and her piety sustained his. She was practical, wise, thoughtful, and highly musical.[4]

I like to think that Adam's appreciation for his new helper increased as he showed his wife God's wonderful creation—for indeed he knew that she was God's special gift to him. Instead of awe and gratefulness, many men today tend to continually compare their wives to other women rather than accepting them as a special gift from God. Where there are areas of growth, husbands should seize the responsibility of encouraging their wives to mature in Christ and to reach their full potential as a wife and mother. So men, don't be bitter towards your wives (Col. 3:19), love and cherish them (Eph. 5:28-29) and appreciate them as God's unique and special gift to you. *"Whoso findeth a wife findeth a good thing, and obtaineth favour of the LORD" (Prov. 18:22).*

What a finale to the week of creation! Stars were spoken into existence; oceans were puddled up, and the dust of the earth burst forth into life. But, it was the creation of woman and the gift of companionship to man, which concluded His work-week!

What is Headship?

But I would have you know that the head of every man is Christ; and the head of the woman is the man; and the head of Christ is God. —1 Corinthians 11:3

How much time do you expend each day in learning how to walk, or to eat, or to sleep? Hopefully, none! These activities are elementary to us and do not need to be learned again and again, unless there has been mental or physical injury to the body. This is the sense in which Paul is explaining the principle of headship in the above verse. The word "know" (*eido*) means "to perceive or discern" in the "perfect tense." Paul wants the Corinthians (and us) to once and for all discern this truth about headship—it should never have to be relearned.

It is obvious from the context of the passage that Paul is referring to authority and not to physical heads on bodies. The teaching focuses on the subject of position and submission within God's created order. There is both a positional order and a relational order throughout God's creation; this is especially true within the marriage union.

Positional order has at its pinnacle, God, then it descends to angelic beings, humanity, animals and the rest of nature (Heb. 1:6-8; 2:6-8; Gen. 1:28-29). In positional order, God and Christ are equal, and the man (reflecting all of the male gender) and the woman (reflecting all of the female gender) are equal. Yet, in relationship order, Jesus Christ (the Son of God) is in subjection to His Father. It is paramount to understand that Jesus Christ is not inferior to God the Father in any way, but He is in submission to the Father. His submission serves as the ultimate example for all believers to pattern their lives after. Jesus Christ is the head of the Church—the supreme authority of all Christians (Eph.1:22, 4:15; Col.1:18). Thus, the Christian must submit to Him and to the various delegated authorities He has arranged over us. In the same way that Christ demonstrates subjection to His Father, the woman is to be in subjection to the man. Subjection is not an affront to equality, but the splendour of divine order.

Submission to authority and role are vital components to any devised order. Can you imagine the chaos that would follow if proper order were not followed in our society? What if people decided traffic signals were to be completely ignored for the sake of expediting travel? What if everyone decided waiting lines at amusement parks, sporting events, the post office, and check-out stands were to be ignored to ensure the quickest possible conclusion of the matter at hand? Normally, one picks up a phone directory knowing that within moments the name, address and telephone number of anyone being searched for will be obtained. However, what if Mr. Johnson, Mrs. Smith, and Miss Jones complained to the phone company about being listed in the middle or towards the end of the telephone directory and demanded to be listed on the first page of the publication next year. Before long, order would be lost, and the usefulness of the directory would be forfeited. Our whole society is based on submission to the order that has been invoked through civil law and social norms. Order is necessary for productivity and blessing; thus, order is at the centre of God's nature. *"For God is not the author of confusion, but of peace ..." (1 Cor. 14:33).*

Submission to order includes dependence on the authority over you. God funnels blessings from heaven through proper channels of authority. All of us are under some authority. Since the days of Noah, this has been His tool for teaching human submission to Himself. The Church is dependent upon Christ for provision and blessing. The Lord Jesus, during His earthly ministry, was dependent upon the Father. A wife is to be dependent upon her husband to provide for her needs and to protect her.

Consequently, the term "head" (in 1 Cor. 11:3) refers to someone who has authority and, thus, the one to whom subjection is to be yielded. G. Morrish states that this meaning is in keeping with the Jewish use of the term in the Septuagint and in the other passages of the New Testament.[1] According to the American Heritage Dictionary, the term "headship" simply refers to "the position or office of the head or leader."[2] This is the general explanation of headship, but its application includes many different spheres of authority. The Bible acknowledges proper headship within three main dimensions of authority: church order, home order, and civil order. Each of these spheres, however, should be in adherence to the overall divine order Paul has spoken of if the maximum blessing of God is to be obtained.

In "Home Order," wives are to be submissive to their husbands (Tit. 2:5; 1 Cor. 11:3; Col. 3:18; 1 Pet. 3:1; Eph. 5:22; Gen. 3:16). Positionally, the wife is equal to her husband, yet God has given the husband authority over the wife in the marital relationship. It was God who designed and initiated the marriage relationship in Genesis 2:23-24; therefore, His rules apply. The Lord Jesus confirmed that God's order for marriage had not changed (Matt. 19:5-6). God does not change (Mal. 3:6; Heb. 13:8); therefore, His order for family life does not change either. Paul explains the "why" of family order in 1 Tim. 2:11-14:

> *Let a woman learn in silence with all submission. And I do not permit a woman to teach or to have authority over a man, but to be in silence. For Adam was formed first, then Eve. And Adam was not deceived, but the woman being deceived, fell into transgression* (NKJV).

Just prior to explaining why the first man was placed in authority over the first woman, the general principle of headship is presented in verses 11 and 12. Adam was created first, and the woman was created from Adam. Therefore, the woman cannot be superior to one that she was taken from. Secondly, the woman was deceived when Satan tempted her, thus, proving that she was not a fit leader for the marital union. Adam, however, sinned with his eyes open. He knew it was wrong, but was inclined to follow his wife's lead.

William MacDonald comments on verse 12 of this passage:

> Neither is a woman to have authority over a man. That means that she must not have dominion over a man, but is to be in silence or quietness. Perhaps we should add that the latter part of this verse is by no means limited to the local assembly. It is a fundamental principle in God's dealings with humankind that man has been given the headship and the woman is in the place of subjection. This does not mean that she is inferior; that is certainly not true. But it does mean that it is contrary to God's will that the woman should have authority or dominion over the man.[3]

Concerning "Civil Order", God never anointed a woman to be a national prophet, priest, or king in Israel. Perhaps Deborah, at a quick glance, would be the closest breech of this statement, but a more detailed observation reveals several important aspects of Deborah's ministry. J. Hunter notes:

> It must be stressed that her [Deborah's] judgeship was different from that of the male judges. Judges 2:18 brings before us three characteristics concerning judges: firstly, the Lord raised them up; secondly, His presence was with them; thirdly, God delivered Israel out of the hand of their enemies all the days of the judge. Of Deborah, Judges 4:4 says she judged Israel "at that time". The previous verse (v. 3) explains this expression. She judged Israel during the "twenty years he (Sisera) mightily oppressed the children of Israel." She judged during the time of bondage, whereas the male judges delivered Israel and ruled over them. Verse 5 then informs us that the children of Israel came to her for judgment, thus availing themselves of her knowledge, wisdom and discernment. When the time came to deliver Israel, God used Barak in the public action and victory, although he was inspired by Deborah. Note also in Heb. 11:32 it is Barak that is named.[4]

So, was Deborah a national leader? No. Deborah imparted wisdom and judgment on an "individual" basis for those who came to her for counsel. She was not a "national" deliverer like the other judges—she did not lead the army into battle against the Canaanites. She herself understood her calling and, thus, encouraged Barak to lead the campaign.

Lastly, "Church Order" also reflects the divine order of headship. Only men were called to be Apostles of the early Church, and only men qualify to be church leaders (elders) of the local assembly (Tit. 1:6; 1 Tim. 3:1-2). Only men are to be duly appointed to the office of deacon in the local church (1 Tim. 3:11-12; Acts 6:3). Only men are to speak in public meetings of the church (1 Cor. 14:34; 1 Tim. 2:9-12). It is not to say that women are not important to the church, for many are mentioned in Scripture as being helpers, encouragers, and even teachers. But what did they teach and to whom? Women taught other women and children in domestic issues of life (Tit. 2:3-4; 2 Tim. 1:5; 3:14-15).

J. Allen emphasizes that there is grammatical evidence to properly translate 1 Timothy 2:12 as "I permit not a woman to be a teacher".[5] K. Wuest, known for his expanded translation of the Bible, mentions the same grammatical support concerning this verse:

> The kind of teacher Paul has in mind is spoken of in Acts 13:2, 1 Cor. 12:28-29, and Ephesians 4:11, God-called, and God equipped teachers, recognized by the Church as those having authority in the Church in matters of doctrine and interpretation. [6]

Women were not to exercise authority over men, nor were the sisters to teach doctrine to the brothers. Perhaps one of the best illustrations of this headship principle in the early church is the narrative account of Paul's return to Jerusalem in Acts 21.

Paul was refreshing himself in the home of Philip for a few days before travelling to Jerusalem. Acts 21:9 records the fact that Philip had four virgin daughters who prophesied. Although it is true that these women had the gift of prophecy, there is no evidence they ever used this gift in the church meetings. Prophecy is not limited to church meetings anymore than prayer is. It should also be pointed out that God used an older male prophet, Agabus, who had to travel some 40 miles to exhort Paul, instead of using Philip's daughters who were not only in the same city, but within the same house that Paul was staying. It would have been much simpler to have one of Philip's daughters rebuke Paul, instead God summoned Agabus. This demonstrates the principle of divine headship. It would have broken God's order to have a woman instruct the Apostle. The fact that prophecy is not constrained to the church meeting is apparent in that Agabus prophesied to Paul outside of a church meeting.

The thoughts of C. H. Mackintosh will conclude our discussion on the women's role in God's order:

> In conclusion, then dear friend, we would just express our ever deepening conviction that *home* is, pre-eminently, the woman's sphere. There she can shine whether as a wife, a mother, or a mistress [home manager], to the glory of Him who has called her to fill those holy relationships. There the most lovely traits of female character are developed—traits which are completely defaced when she abandons her home work and enters the domain of the public preacher. We believe it is plainly opposed to Scripture for a woman to speak in the Church, or to teach, or in any way, usurp authority over the man. But if there be a meeting of a private, social character, there is, in our judgment, an opening for the free communication of the thought, provided always that the woman keep the place assigned her by the voice of nature and the Word of God. [7]

Marital Companionship

Though God desires godly children through the marriage union of a man and a woman (Mal. 2:15), His overshadowing aspiration for marriage was intimate companionship. By entering into a marriage covenant, a man and a woman become companions for life in God's best plan. Since the marriage covenant initiates blessed camaraderie between a man and a woman as husband and wife, we pause to examine the biblical meaning of marital companionship by evaluating the two Hebrew words used in the Old Testament to speak of the marriage partner or companion.

The prophet Malachi harshly rebuked the men of Israel for divorcing their wives (Mal. 2:11-14). He informed them of God's anger over the matter, for *"He hates divorce"* (Mal. 2:16 NKJV), and of His forthcoming judgment upon them for their negligent behaviour. Malachi 2:14 reads *"Yet ye say, Wherefore [Why]? Because the LORD hath been witness between thee and the wife of thy youth, against whom thou hast dealt treacherously: yet is she thy **companion**, and the wife of thy covenant."* The Hebrew word for companion, *chabereth*, means "a consort or wife," but its root word *chaber* means "to be associated with or united to" or "to be knit together." We conclude that one aspect of companionship is a sense of duty and a commitment to stay knitted together. It is interesting that the modern Hebrew word for marriage, *kiddushin*, means "sanctification" (being set apart). The marriage bond "sets apart" a husband and wife to fulfill a lifetime covenant of intimate and committed companionship before God. A marriage must be based on a forged commitment of both parties to stay together no matter what. Not only is the mindset of staying together a necessity for a marriage to thrive, but it is one of the greatest gifts to pass along to your children.

Solomon rebukes an adulterous wife in Proverbs 2:17, *"Which forsaketh the **guide** (companion or partner) of her youth, and forgetteth the covenant of her God."* The Hebrew word for guide, *alluwph*, means "to be familiar and intimate, with a foremost friend." Another key aspect of the marriage covenant is intimacy, a deep desire to disclose and to be familiar with one another. If your spouse is not your best friend, you are missing God's design for marriage.

Biblical companionship, therefore, consists of an unwavering duty of *commitment* and open disclosure that promotes *intimacy*. When will a marriage relationship be the most satisfying? When total commitment leads to open disclosure. Full disclosure promotes exuberant passion being shared between a husband and wife. Jehovah's passion for Israel—his wife through covenant—is poetically described in Ezekiel 16:8: *"Now when I passed by thee, and looked upon thee, behold, thy time was the time of **love**; and I spread my skirt over thee, and covered thy nakedness: yea, I sware unto thee, and entered into a covenant with thee, saith the Lord God, and thou becamest mine."* The Hebrew word for "love" in this verse is *dowd*, meaning "to boil" (i.e. figuratively: "to love" and, by implication, "a lover"). This word is rendered "love" seven times in the Old Testament and always confers the sense of a boiling pot of fervent passion between a man and a woman (not necessarily sexually).

If a marriage relationship is pursued and obtained on the basis of romantic love instead of obligation and disclosure, no foundation will be present to weather life's storms. However, a marriage based on commitment and intimacy will be joyfully romantic. This was God's intention for marital companionship! No reason exists for a Christian marriage not to achieve biblical companionship. As a husband aspires to biblical manhood by the grace of God and a wife pursues scriptural femininity by the grace of God, a joyful companionship will be the result.

Marital companionship cannot displace our fellowship with God, for marital bliss is wholly dependent upon our communion with God. A Christian marriage must draw nigh to Christ to thrive. Whether man or woman, the Lord Jesus said our relationship with Him has first priority: *"Thou shalt love the Lord thy God with all thy heart, and with all thy soul, and with all thy mind"* (Matt. 22:37). The Lord <u>must</u> be our first love, or we will lack the wherewithal to serve Him with the proper motives and intensity. Ultimately, as the church of Ephesus learned (Rev. 2:4), a believer will lose his or her testimony if Christ is not foremost in his or her devotion. Paul exhorted the church at Colosse not to have divided or multiplied endearments, but to have *one affection*—Christ: *"Set your affection on things above, not on things on the earth" (Col. 3:2).*

After Christ, the spouse is to receive second preference of devotion. By a marriage covenant, a man and woman enter into a lifetime commitment with each other (Mal. 2:14-16; Matt. 19:5-6). Though the wife may often be focused upon attending to her children, her love for her husband is never supplanted by her love for her children. The Christian wife entered into an eternal covenant when she accepted Jesus Christ as Lord and Saviour; the New Covenant is sealed by the redeeming blood of Christ. She commenced a life-long covenant with her husband through marriage, yet no *vows* to love and serve her children are required by God. As children are a heritage and gift from God (Ps. 127:3), a natural stewardship is assumed, but no maternal oaths are necessary. When the children are grown, they will leave father and mother and cleave to another, unless God has called them to singleness. A good mother will pour her heart and soul into her children, but she will never lose sight of her first love—the Lord Jesus—and her lifetime companion— her husband.

·It is interesting that Paul reflects this order of family precedence in addressing the woman's relationship to her husband and children throughout Scripture. The husband is always mentioned first and then the children (Tit. 2:4; Col. 3:18-20; Eph. 5:33-6:1). When higher priorities of ministry have been met (Christ, husband, and children), other Christians can then be served (Rom. 12:10, 1 Pet. 4:7-10). These priorities are important for the edification of the church, the body of Christ, *but only if the family is not neglected.* The Apostle Paul addresses a final priority of service in Romans 12. First, he speaks of ministering to other saints (Rom. 12:9-16), then to unsaved neighbors and one's enemies (Rom. 12:17-21).

It is understood that a crying baby may interrupt a mother's quiet time with the Lord or a phone call from a hurting friend may infringe upon a moment of marital intimacy, but the focus of this discussion is not on the uncontrollable facets of life but on the balance of daily ministry priorities. Both husbands and wives should view every activity they embark upon from an eternal perspective: What matters for eternity? What value does this activity have in enhancing the kingdom of God? Many shipwrecked families have navigated about the dangerous shoals of worldliness, but have fallen prey to the hidden reefs of good ministries. Beware of the rigorous undercurrent of self-ambition and the wind of human manipulation. Without course corrections, your family may find itself hopelessly run aground in some legitimate service.

My wife returned home from a ladies' Bible conference a few years ago with a practical illustration of the above-mentioned priorities. As she was sharing some of her conference gleanings with me, she paused for a moment, posed a curious smirk, and proceeded to proclaim, "And you are my second nut!" She then explained to me the illustration that related to her comment. The speaker had taken a pint canning jar and filled it full of rice. She then took four walnuts and explained that the first one represented the Lord, the second depicted one's husband, the third symbolized one's children, and the fourth nut portrayed all remaining relationships. With great pressure, she attempted to push the first walnut into the jar, but, of course, no capacity was available within the jar to receive the nut. The teacher went on to explain that the wife and mother was represented by the jar. If she chose to fill her existence with "the fluff of life," or unprioritized activities (the rice), she would not have room for the relationships that really mattered.

Next, the speaker emptied the jar and placed the first nut in it (representing her relationship with God). Then, the second nut (symbolizing her relationship with her husband) was added. With ample space still available, the third walnut (her relationship with her children) was inserted, and finally, the fourth nut reflecting the wife's relationship with Christians and non-believers found just enough room within the jar. After all of the walnuts were in the jar, the teacher poured in a bit of rice, which settled into some accessible space around them. The application? When a woman empties herself of selfish ambitions and actively pursues divine order in her life, she will have sufficient room for her Lord, her husband, her children and her brothers and sisters in the Lord as well as others in need. The Lord gives perfect grace for everything *He desires* to be accomplished every day. If you are perpetually frazzled and ragged day in and day out, review your priorities to ensure that you are not out of the will of God.

With biblical priorities in view, let us review the cultural travesty that is presently facing the sanctum of marriage. From the period of the honeymoon to the first diaper, the wife has much of herself available to serve the Lord and her husband, provided a career, other friendships, and general busyness are not draining away her capacity.

Remember those newborn days? Tough, right? The newborn's arrival at home is a joyful time, but it also can be a stressful experience. The baby cries often, and mom eventually becomes weary and fatigued. She yearns for sleep and a break from the daily routine. To add further complications to this happy home, dad is grappling with the independent aspects of motherhood upon which he cannot intrude. Because much of his wife's energy is focused upon the wee one, he may feel left out and wrongly conclude that a loss of intimacy is occurring in the marriage, as his wife's availability for companionship and capacity to express affection to him have been diminished.

The marriage must adjust so that it is able to satisfy both the needs of a newborn and the need of marital companionship. The husband who feels slighted by maternal duties cannot sublimate his need for companionship in a career, in other relationships, or in the acquiring of new "toys." He must continually reorient his thinking about intimacy and be innovative in exploring new avenues to emotionally bond with his wife. As home life changes, the marriage relationship must adjust to maintain active companionship.

I recall both the excitement and the disappointment of our first child's arrival. Seeing the birth of your first child is one of the mountaintop experiences of life; yet, I distinctly remember the feeling that I had lost a part of my wife forever—

motherhood had stolen it from me. In time, I realized, however, that I was being selfish and that my wife was simply fulfilling God's design for her. Marriage does not become better or worse with the advent of children; it just becomes much different! Children bring unique opportunities for couples to explore new depths of marital admiration, devotion, and service.

An unfortunate situation often occurs when couples enter into parenthood with the husband seeking selfish gratification through new vices. Consequently, the wife receives less love and support from her husband, which erodes the foundation of companionship in the marriage. In response, the wife tends to satisfy her intimacy shortfall by developing deeper emotional connections with her children and other women, further reducing her need for fellowship with her husband. The rift gradually widens until one day, while lingering in bed, your mate rolls over towards you, and you hesitate, perhaps only for a moment, before shaking from your mind the question, "Who is this person?", yet it was there long enough to be heard.

It is important for husbands not to drift in their responsibility to initiate love during those newborn days—in doing so, they strengthen the marriage relationship instead of allowing an emotional rift to be realized. If a husband does not choose to impart extra emotional support to his wife during the child bearing and rearing years, the very bundles of joy God bestowed upon the marital union may conceivably wedge it apart later. The solemn vow of "until death do us part" does not include the exception clause "until children do us part." Both spouses have the responsibility to not allow it to happen. God's design for marriage consists of a life-long pursuit of companionship which includes an unwavering commitment and full disclosure as its basis.

To Marry or Not?

Next to salvation, the determination to marry or not is likely the most important decision of one's entire life. Homes, jobs, institutions of learning, friends, and investments will come and go, but God's design for marriage is for life! Of course, the next question, "Whom to marry?", is equally important if one determines that marriage is God's plan for their life. In his book *The Disciple's Manual*, William MacDonald sums up this matter concisely:

> Marriage is God's general rule for the human race. An exception is found in Matthew 19:12—there are some who are eunuchs for the kingdom's sake. These people are willing to forego marriage in order to give themselves without distraction to the work of the Lord.[1]

Concerning service to the Lord, each individual must decide if he or she can better serve the Lord single or as a married couple. Some ministries are more suited to singles, while others require a married couple. While on a recent mission trip in Mexico, the local missionary warned our group of young people not to pursue missionary work in his area as a single person. He said, "Single missionaries cause too many difficulties in the work here, and many of the local people will not accept mixed marriages." He warned them, "If you come to help us long term—come married." For this very reason, Jim and Elisabeth

Elliot married—it enabled them to serve the Lord better in foreign missionary work than they could have separately.

Yet, in a different case, a single man I know served the Lord on a remotely located ranch specifically designed to minister to troubled boys (adolescent delinquents). His unmarried state allowed him more availability and flexibility to maintain order and accountability among the occupants. Many have chosen the self-sacrificing avenue of single service: John Darby, Robert Chapman, Fanny Crosby, Amy Carmichael, Gladys Aylward, Corrie Ten Boom, Mary Slessor, and William MacDonald to name a few.

Pertaining to the subject of singleness, Paul wrote:

He that is unmarried careth for the things that belong to the Lord, how he may please the Lord: But he that is married careth for the things that are of the world, how he may please his wife. There is difference also between a wife and a virgin. The unmarried woman careth for the things of the Lord, that she may be holy both in body and in spirit: but she that is married careth for the things of the world, how she may please her husband. —1 Corinthians 7:32-34

Warren Wiersbe provides the following comments to Paul's statement:

Once again, Paul emphasized living for the Lord. He did not suggest that it was impossible for a man or a woman to be married and serve God acceptably, because we know too many people who have done it. But the married servant of God must consider his or her mate, as well as the children God may give them; and this could lead to distraction. It is a fact of history that both John Wesley and George Whitefield might have been better off had they remained single—Wesley's wife finally left him, and Whitefield travelled so much that his wife was often alone for long periods of time. [The author notes that Whitefield married, at least in part, because he had witnessed the godly home of Jonathan Edwards and was deeply impressed by the far-reaching spiritual impact his home had in furthering the kingdom of God].

It is possible to please both the Lord and your mate, if you are yielded to Christ and obeying the Word. Many of us have discovered that a happy home and satisfying marriage are a wonderful encouragement in the difficulties of Christian service. A well-known Scottish preacher was experiencing a great deal of public criticism because of a stand he took on a certain issue, and almost every day there was a negative report in the newspapers. A friend met him one day and asked, "How are you able to carry on in the face of this opposition?" The man replied quietly, "I am happy at home."[2]

Each unmarried believer must examine his or her own heart to determine if marriage will help or hinder his or her service to the Lord. Each Christian has his or her own gift and calling from God and must be obedient to His Word. Those who serve in singleness have fewer family distractions, and those who serve married provide each other mutual encouragement in the work—both conditions have their place in the kingdom of God.

If a believer discerns that he or she does not have the gift of singleness and that it would be better to serve the Lord married, he or she must then be careful to wed a spiritually-minded mate who shares the same calling to serve God. If one weds, it is understood that he or she cannot neglect their domestic responsibilities for the sake of ministry. Many missionaries and gospel preachers in the 19th century won hundreds of thousands to Christ but lost their own families to the world because of neglect. Though a staunch prohibitionist and successful itinerant gospel preacher, Billy Sunday's own heart was broken because two of his four children were alcoholics. While he was spending prolonged years exploring uncharted regions of Africa's interior, David Livingstone's family was living in poverty in England. After one four-year absence, Livingstone's wife went looking for the pioneer missionary, but her desired reunion never came for she contracted malaria in the jungles of Africa and died before ever finding her husband.

Has God conferred on you the gift of singleness to serve Him unhindered by family responsibilities? Because of the difficult ministry God had appointed to Jeremiah, he was *forbidden* to take a wife (Jer. 16:2). Some ministries are only for singles, yet Paul recognized that God's natural design is for humankind to marry, unless He specifically calls an individual to a single's ministry. *"It is good for a man not to touch a woman. Nevertheless, to avoid fornication, let every man have his own wife" (1 Cor. 7:1-2).* Paul desired believers not to be hindered by family responsibilities in ministry, but realized that singleness was not the norm in Christian service.

For those without the gift of singleness, selection of a marriage partner is the most important decision of one's life, next to salvation, and waiting for God's provision is one of the most exhausting exercises of one's faith, especially for women. An anticipating sister writes of the lingering trial:

This is really a frustrating thing for a lot of single women. They have believed all their life that God's plan for them was to be a wife and mother. They don't feel they have the mysterious "gift of singleness" that so many preachers speak of. Rather, they wait year in and year out to *"be found" (Prov. 18:22).* Many of my girlfriends in their late 20s, 30s, and 40s have prayed for years that the Lord would show them if He is calling them to a single ministry—but He doesn't seem to (Maybe we aren't listening or don't want to hear?). It doesn't feel like a choice or a call for most singles ... it feels more like a life of waiting. Why am I not married?"

Statistically speaking, population demographics provide some insight as to why many women who desire to marry remain single. The U.S. Census Bureau reported in 2003 that there were about 4.4 percent more females than males in the United States.[3] United Nations population data reveals a similar gender trend in Canada with approximately 1.8 percent more females residing there than males.[4] In general, most nations have more females than males, but there are a few exceptions, with China being one of the most notable. China's strict population control laws and gender prejudices have led to a significant increase in the male populace, as compared to the female inhabitants (The UN estimates 5.6 percent more males than females for the year 2005.).[5]

The gender demographics seem to directly relate to gender longevity statistics, which affirm that women live longer than men. HHS Centres for Disease Control and Prevention document that life expectancy for men in the US increased to 74.4 years in 2001; for women, however the life expectancy increased to 79.8 years for the same year.[6] So far we have learned that there are more females than males in the US because males do not live as long as females, on the average. If males simply died of *old age* sooner than females, there would be nothing gained by this analysis to explain why many women do not marry. But, if males die at a much faster rate than females before and during the typical years that men and women marry, a statistical reason for many single women not marrying would then exist.

Based on the US Disaster Centre mortality statistics for the year 1996, the following is noted. The male to female death rate for ages: 0 to 9 years was 1.29; 10 to 19 years was 2.35; 20 to

29 years was 2.83; and for 30 to 39 years was 2.19. In fact, the male/female death rate ratio does not drop below one until men and women are over 80 years of age.[7] Though males and females enter into the world at approximately the same rate, males exit the world at a much faster rate throughout their normal life expectancy. Males tend to be more curious (especially in the early years), more aggressive, and more likely to risk their lives in thrill-seeking ventures than females—the cost to them is often death. If you have high school students who are driving, you already know that the insurance companies are very aware of these statistics, as auto insurance for young males is normally much higher than for females of the same age.

So why do many women, who desire to be wed, never marry? There are several possible reasons, but one obvious explanation is that many potential husbands have died before having the opportunity to marry. Statistically speaking, there just are not enough men for every woman to have a husband.

Besides the gender mortality rate reality, the believing woman is further constrained by husband availability, as she is only to marry a Christian man (2 Cor. 6:14; 1 Cor. 7:39). Unfortunately, the desire to marry is so strong that some women professing Christ will forsake the Lord in order to obtain an unbelieving husband. The Apostle Paul acknowledges that the same travesty was apparent in his day (1 Tim. 5:11-12).

What is to be the proper attitude of those desiring to be married? Proverbs 18:22 reads *"Whoso **findeth** a wife findeth a good thing, and obtaineth favour of the Lord."* **Those who look to get married usually do!** However, the individual who waits on the Lord to provide a spouse will *find* him or her (that is if God intends for them to marry), and it will be obvious to all parties concerned that the Lord is in the matter.

John Calvin summarized our propensity to run ahead of the Lord, "The evil in our desire typically does not lie in what we want, but in that we want it too much." For many, "to wait" feels like "weight." Be patient, and allow God to work in your life. You don't want to marry just anyone but God's best—for some, this undoubtedly will be God Himself. The Lord does not consider single women to be "second class" citizens of heaven, nor should the Church. All those redeemed by the blood of Christ deserve equality of love and ministry—unmarried women are often ignored and excluded from hospitality.

Each of us must determine whether we have the gift of singleness, and those of us who don't have it must wait upon the Lord's provision. God's marital blessing is obtained in "finding" not "looking."

For those "maids in waiting," perhaps the following practical guidelines will add patience and wisdom to your anticipation and assist you in demonstrating godly femininity while single:

1. Don't create categories of single brothers in your mind. You know what I mean: "he's promising;" "he has possibilities;" and "I would rather die." The Lord might just surprise you and occasion the very impossibility you determined in your own mind! Adopt a sister mentality relationship to all the brethren. This will help keep you from being blinded by your own flesh and assist you in recognizing God's provision for you, when, and if, He does provide a husband.

2. Don't thumb your nose at a single man who attempts to serve and protect you. It is the natural ministry of men to lead and protect women; the outworking of a good shepherd will be witnessed long before he has a flock of his own. The same is true of elders in the local church. So, if a brother (whom you know and trust) wants to escort

you to your car, which is parked in the north forty of a huge lot, allow him to do so. There may be a brother who shows good spiritual wisdom and leadership—accept and appreciate his counsel in your decision making. He is not in authority over you, so don't allow him to rule you, but he may assist and encourage you.

> A real woman understands that man was created to be the initiator, and she operates on the premise, this is primarily a matter of attitude. I am convinced that the woman who understands and accepts with gladness the difference between masculine and feminine will be, without pretense or self-consciousness, womanly.
>
> —Elisabeth Elliot

3. Continue to learn about God's general plan for the woman: keeping the home, motherhood, and being a helper and companion to her husband. As you grow in appreciation for God's order in the home and His safeguards for you, you will naturally be better mentally prepared for the exhausting ministry of a wife and mother, if this is God's specific design for your life.

4. Cultivate godly character and inward beauty in your life. This is addressed more fully in a later chapter. It suffices here to merely say, "what you win a man with is what you win him to." If you resort to flesh, either through manipulation or flaunting your womanly features to lure a husband, don't be surprised if your marriage constantly wrestles with the flesh. Men have a general weakness to be stimulated by visual imagery and, thus, to be stumbled in their thought life, so don't add to their misery. However, if you portray genuine feminine beauty as God

recognizes it, you will likely and unknowingly attract the attention of a godly man who thinks the way God does concerning womanhood. What is beautiful feminine character? Chaste conduct, godly fear, and a meek and quiet spirit (1 Pet. 3:2-4). Dear sisters, you want a husband who will love you for who you are not what you won't be in ten years. *"For which cause we faint not; but though our outward man perish, yet the inward man is renewed day by day" (2 Cor. 4:16).* The outward perishes so win them to something that should only get better!

5. Recognize that God's transfer of authority over you is His protection for you. God's rule for marriage has not changed since the first couple was married (Matt. 19:5); *"For this cause shall a man leave father and mother, and shall cleave to his wife: and they twain* [the two] *shall be one flesh."* One cannot say that this is the Law, because this mandate was declared at the beginning, before the Mosaic Law was given. Marriage is an institution that is unchanged throughout the Bible. It seems that Adam was awakened to his need for a companion through performing the work God had assigned him (naming the animals who were likely in pairs). After Adam was awakened to his need, he was put to sleep and then awakened to learn that the One in authority over him had provided a woman for his need. Single people should remain in happy fellowship with their parents (who are hopefully believers) and heed their counsel in this important matter of marriage. Ultimately, it is the bride and groom that consent to marry, but if it is the mind of the Lord, all those who are spiritually-

minded and in authority over the young couple will be in one accord.

In the Bible, we don't see good examples of children getting married when they want to and to whom they want. Children are *given in marriage* when they are ready (Matt. 22:30; 24:38; Mark 12:25; Luke 17:27; 20:34-35). The phrase normally is applied to daughters, but we understand that parental authority is over their sons also: Matthew 22:2; *"a certain king, which made a marriage for his son."* Abraham initiated in picking a wife for Isaac; Judah took a wife for Er, and Jehoiada took wives for the King Joash. Sons *leave* to establish themselves as new family heads, but daughters are *given* in marriage. *"The fire consumed their young men; and their maidens were **not given to marriage**" (Ps. 78:63). "So then he that **giveth her in marriage** doeth well" (1 Cor. 7:38).*

A son will *leave* his father's authority to establish a new family head. He will then be joined to a wife; he will "cleave" to her, and a new family is begun. In this way, *she experiences a transfer of authority* (her father's to her husband's). This transition of authority is clearly stated in Numbers 30:3-16 in that a father could nullify his daughter's vow to God (if living under his authority), or a husband could nullify his wife's vow to God. This transfer of authority may explain why, when Paul explains divine order in 1 Corinthians 11:3, the woman is nestled between Christ and the man.

It is apparent from Scripture that daughters lived at home and under parental authority until they were wed.

Scripture contains no example of any young maiden leaving her father's home and authority to pursue a life on her own. The man was created as an "initiator" and the woman as a "responder," so it is hazardous for a single woman to be in the world without the protection of godly authority. Jacob's daughter Dinah, who was raped by Shechem, learned this matter the hard way (Gen. 34). A father is his daughter's protector until she is bound to a husband or she seeks to serve the Lord as a single beyond the sphere of his presence. In such cases where her father cannot protect her, either a godly oversight of elders or a godly older couple (e.g. a missionary couple) would watch over and care for her.

We speak of a scriptural principle here and not a command, as it is understood that, practically speaking, this protective authority will be hard to implement at times. Yet, Scripture widely demonstrates the principle. Consider the following examples: (1) Ruth remained under the authority of Naomi, who had become the head of her home after the death of her husband. Ruth realized a transition of authority from Naomi to Boaz through marriage (Ruth 3:1; 4:13). (2) It is likely that the parents of Mary and Martha were deceased as they are not mentioned in Scripture, yet they apparently lived with their brother Lazarus (John 11:1), who, in the absence of the parental authority, would naturally watch over his sisters. (3) Some converted women, such as Mary Magdalene, apparently were brought directly under the authority and protection of the Lord and His disciples. These women travelled with the Lord and ministered directly to Him. (Luke 8:2-3; 23:49). (4) Paul commends

Phoebe, a faithful sister in the Lord's service, to the care of the local church in Rome (Rom. 16:1-2).

If, for some reason, a daughter leaves the protection of her home for schooling or to work, she is still under her father's authority (much like a missionary remains under the authority of the commending assembly). Some Scriptural examples: (1) Zipporah worked in the fields attending the flocks of her father Reuel, but was given to Moses for a wife by her father (Ex. 2:16-21). (2) Rebekah was a virgin living in her father's house but worked throughout the day outside of the home tending the family's sheep until she was given to Isaac for a wife (Gen. 24). (3) Although Esther was taken to the women's court for one year of "beauty treatments," her adopted father Mordecai (Est. 2:7) walked every day to the court of the women's house to encourage her and to check on her. (Est. 2:11). This ceased once she married the king. Mordecai understood that his responsibility for Esther continued until she was married and experienced a transition in authority. This teaching is not popular with worldly trends, but it is God's way!

6. Avoid the "dating game." I have yet to counsel a married couple who have said that the dating experience was profitable for them. Most came away with deep hurts; many lost their virginity, and some have contracted diseases that are incurable. These factors often cause emotional difficulties and feelings of guilt after entering into marriage. It is possible for some to date with integrity and for others to approach courtship with folly, so to avoid wrangling over vague and unscriptural terms, I will simply recommend that you strive to protect your

heart from unneeded hurt. You only want to expose your heart to your spouse, so save your whole self for your life-mate. Ensure that discussions with individuals of the opposite gender are public and discretely supervised by those in authority over you. Have clear boundaries for acceptable conduct with the opposite gender and don't compromise them. If you have unsaved parents, ask the elders in your assembly or a godly older couple you know and trust to look after you.

The above guidelines will protect your heart, help you to walk in integrity with blameless conduct, and better prepare you for marriage, if indeed this is God's plan for you. Yet, these are guidelines—patterns observed from Scripture, not rigid commands. God's best plan for marriage is one man and one woman, bound by a covenant for life. The process of obtaining a spouse will be unique for each individual, but it is my earnest opinion that when we stray from scriptural patterns, which were given for our learning (1 Cor. 10:6), the likelihood of a failed or unhappy marriage is greatly increased. God's authority is like a big funnel through which He passes down blessings to us. Let us all stay under His authority, as unto the Lord. When we disobey God's order, we don't remove ourselves from authority; we simply place ourselves under Satan's authority and, thus, suffer the loss of God's fellowship and blessing.

Hudson Taylor supplies an excellent example of heeding God's authority in the matter of marriage. While serving the Lord in China, Taylor determined to allow the Lord to resolve the matter of marriage in his own life. Taylor had met a fine Christian woman, Miss Dyer, whom he felt the Lord would have him marry in order to serve Him better in China. But, there was a problem: an older woman who had been entrusted with the care of Miss Dyer had absolutely forbidden the two of them from developing a relationship. Taylor's methods for reaching the Chinese people with the gospel were not favoured by most missionaries at that time; consequently, the missionary community was hostile towards him. His crime? He dressed like the Chinese and lived among them. Taylor honoured her authority and request, but also told her that he would be writing to the uncle of Miss Dyer who was her legal guardian (both of her parents were dead). Given the sea travel of the day, he expected to wait some four to five months to receive a response. While he was waiting, Taylor wrote in his journal:

> I have never known disobedience to the definite command of a parent, even if that parent were mistaken, that was not followed by retribution. Conquer through the Lord. He can open any door. The responsibility is with the parent in such a case, and it is a great one. When son or daughter can say in all sincerity, "I am waiting for you, Lord, to open the door," the matter is in His hands, and He will take it up. ... We need Him to direct our steps. Nay more, we need to pass through this wilderness leaning, always leaning on our Beloved. May we in reality do this, and all will be well.[8]

The uncle of Miss Dyer thoroughly researched Hudson Taylor and found him to be a man of integrity and well esteemed in London. He consented to the marriage on the condition that Miss Dyer be of proper age (21). They had to wait only two months before marrying. Taylor had waited upon the Lord instead of resorting to baser means of resolving the issue, and God had marvelously answered his prayer. The Taylors had seven children in China, and Mrs. Taylor, though taken home early in life, was a great helper in the missionary work there.

The marital pursuits of John Wesley serve as a warning that even spiritually-minded people can adopt fickle thinking and erratic methods in choosing a mate. Gary Inrig offers a synopsis of Wesley's marital endeavours:

> When John Wesley was thirty-two years old, he was a bachelor missionary in the colony of Georgia. While he was serving a church in Savannah, he met a young woman named Sophie Christina Hopkey. She was pretty and intelligent, and Wesley fell head over heels in love with her. But Wesley belonged to a group called the Holy Club, and one of their ideals was that members should remain single. So Wesley was caught in a dilemma. Was it the will of God for him to marry Sophie or not? To find out, he and a friend named Charles Delamotte decided to draw lots. On three pieces of paper they wrote: "Marry"; "Think not of it this year"; and "Think of it no more." Then they put the pieces in a container. Delamotte closed his eyes and drew out the third one, "Think of it no more." Wesley was heartbroken, but he took the result to be the will of God. He ended the courtship, and, not long after, he sailed back to England. In his journal, he wrote over the record of his romance, "Snatched as a brand out of the fire!"

> Shortly after his return to England, Wesley came to saving faith in the Lord Jesus, and he began the evangelistic ministry which God used so greatly. During his travels, he fell in love with another woman, a widow and a Bible class teacher named Grace Murray. This time he tried a different approach to finding the will of God about marriage. He listed seven factors he desired in a wife—her roles as "Housekeeper, Nurse, Companion, Friend, and a Fellow Labourer in the Gospel of Christ…, Her Gifts, and the Fruits of her Labours." He set out the pros and cons, and then he stated his conclusion: "Therefore all my seven arguments against marriage are totally set aside. Nay, some of them seem to prove that I ought to marry and that Grace Murray is the person."

Unfortunately, John's brother Charles did not agree. He believed that marriage would hamper John's evangelistic work. When he [John] heard the news, he galloped over to Grace's home, jumped off his horse, ran in, and said to her, "Grace Murray, you have broken my heart!" Then he fainted at her feet. That shook Grace so badly that she hastily married another man. Strike two for Wesley!

Finally, a year and a half later, at the age of forty-seven, John did marry, a wealthy widow named Mary Vazeille. I do not know how Wesley chose her or what Charles had to say, but John made a mistake. He had a very unhappy marriage, and, twenty years later, she left him. When she did, Wesley wrote in his journal, "I have not left her, I would not send her away; I will not recall her."[9]

To marry or to not marry is an important decision, but for the Christian, it is a secondary matter in comparison with his or her determination to yield to Christ. For the believer, marriage should only be contemplated from a mindset of how to better please the Lord. R. C. Chapman, a lifelong bachelor, characterizes the proper attitude of a disciple of Christ in service. Let us ponder and yield!

The Lord Jesus always finds service for willing hearts and willing hands: Let us desire only that service for which He has fitted us. It is a mark of steady progress in the ways of God when a servant of Christ, like his Master, makes no choice of service, seeking only to please his Lord. If by walking before God we rise above the praise of men, we shall not be vexed or disappointed by their disapproval and blame. He that is humble, and ever desiring to serve others, will surely find others desiring to serve him. The joy and triumph of faith are only to be found in the way of unreserved consecration of ourselves to God and diligent service to Christ.[10]

Marital Satisfaction

As Adam and Eve quickly found out, man's fallen nature does not promote intimacy between a husband and wife; sin only separates and causes division. Genesis 3 records how the first marriage was divided by sin. The first family was divided by sin in Genesis 4, and the first society was divided by sin in Genesis 6. Sin divides, separates and causes disorder. After the first couple sinned, they immediately became uncomfortable with each other and tried to conceal themselves from each other. Sin seeks to hide who we are. Every family since that time has felt the same seclusionary effects of sin. Individualism and selfishness tend to smother active intimacy. Husbands and wives must actively oppose these isolating tendencies. A Christ-centreed marriage with good communication will best fend off this natural pitfall. If you are not working to build intimacy in your marriage, you will most likely drift apart!

The information in the following table was compiled by Norman Wright and represents the conclusion of numerous research studies over a fifteen-year period.[1] The table clearly reflects the decline in meaningful companionship many married couples experience through the child-bearing and rearing years. Marital satisfaction is high prior to and after having children in the home. However, in the Christian home, this fallout is avoidable if godly wisdom and counsel are heeded and divine grace is relied upon.

Husbands' and Wives' Marital Satisfaction Over the Family Career

Nine = High Marital Satisfaction   Zero = Low Marital Satisfaction

Couples Newly Established	= 9.0
Couples in Childbearing Period	= 4.9
Families with School Children	= 4.7
Families with Secondary School Children	= 2.9
Families with Young Adults	= 3.5
Aging in the Middle Years	= 7.3
Aging Families	= 6.3

Husbands especially have to work at opening up. Most husbands don't involve their wives closely in their work and/or their ministries. Most wives, however, long to communicate in order to understand this realm of exclusion. Women, on the other hand, tend to speak more than twice as many words a day as men and are typically better connectors with people.

A woman may have many close friends with whom she feels that she can share intimate matters, whereas most men have none or perhaps one. Wives, encourage your husbands to reveal themselves in these exclusionary spheres. Be very careful *to listen and not interrupt*, or you may close the door of disclosure. After you sense your husband has finished expressing himself, promote the conversation to new levels by asking genuine questions or by repeating back to him what he has said to indicate to him that you were listening and do care about what he has said.

My wife and I have been both frustrated and provoked to laughter by the differences in male and female communication. Men think and communicate differently than women do. When telephoning a brother in the Lord about a particular subject, our conversation reminds me of the old television game, *Name that Tune*. In this game, contestants would take turns negotiating the smallest number of musical notes by which a particular tune might be identified. This game is similar to male communication in that the main goal is to use as few words as possible in conversing about the single subject you intend to conquer. Words beyond this task are a waste of time and not practical.

A recent telephone conversation with a sister in the Lord typifies the woman's need for communication. The conversation lasted ten minutes, and I might have uttered only 30 words, which seems to be typical in cross-gender communication. Telephone conversations with men lasting more than three or four minutes are rare for me; however, I am often coerced into a 20 or 30 minute conversation with a female caller (mainly to listen). The practical, but dull, male intellect says, "What was the purpose of that call?", whereas the woman's goal was to more deeply connect with the person she was talking with and, of course, to accomplish any needed items of business, which is often secondary. Sometimes women need to vent by verbalizing their frustrations in order to feel better, while, at other times, they may simply be talking things out to conclude a matter in their mind. Men usually arrive at a conclusion first then declare what it is. Men can become frustrated when they ask their wives a "yes/no" question and get a five-minute response. Even after the lengthy discourse, the husband may still be struggling to understand what the answer actually was or he may be perturbed as to why his wife didn't tell him the conclusion of the matter five minutes earlier. God made men and women different, and we all need to accept, understand, and utilize both genders' intrinsic strengths and diversity in the marriage relationship.

In summary, most women enjoy connecting emotionally with others in conversation; while the need to communicate content may be important, it is usually not primary. Men, on the other hand, are primarily focused on one "mission" at a time and would rather have a tooth pulled than drop their shields and allowing a conversation to penetrate beyond the emotional barrier that protects and conceals their feelings. Men, take the challenge, and share with your wife something you have not confided to her before. Wives, do not share this disclosure with anyone else, or you may not get another opportunity to penetrate so deeply within your husband's thinking. Husbands and wives should be best friends and have full disclosure. A Christian man recently shared with me that he thoroughly enjoyed those occasions when his wife invoked the "silent treatment." When the lack of marital communication becomes the norm or is refreshing to one or both spouses, beware— disaster is nigh!

A final warning to men. We tend to be problem solvers, but there is definitely a wrong time to suggest a solution to your wife's problems. If she is thinking audibly (talking aloud about some worrisome matter) while you just happen to be in the vicinity or if she is just venting internal pressure vocally, be a listening ear. Listening shows love. Don't jump into the dialogue with a three-point plan to resolve her dilemma because that is not what she needs or wants; this course of action will only add to her frustration. Later, after praying about the situation, approach your wife by suggesting a possible means of helping her. "I have been thinking about what you shared with me. What do you think about trying to…?" Solicit her inputs, ensure her ownership in developing a course of action, then pray together over the matter. While this may not be the logical approach for most men, it is the one that will, in general, work the best in building a lasting friendship with your wife.

The Perpetual Problem

Experience in marriage counseling has shown a common scenario that repeatedly inflicts havoc in Christian marriages. Interestingly, this same problematic pattern is shown to us in the Bible. Paul states that the Old Testament narrative is for our learning, so we don't repeat the same mistakes (1 Cor. 10:6). Yet, the agitations within Isaac and Rebekah's marriage are, in my opinion, the most common problem adversely affecting the marriages of Christians today. Let us study the Genesis narrative to glean lessons from the mistakes of others.

Isaac and Rebekah's behaviour at the consummation of their marriage (Gen. 24) is noteworthy. Rebekah dismounted from her camel and covered herself with a veil as an act of *reverence* for Isaac and his authority, while Isaac is said to have *loved* Rebekah. This example is exactly what Paul declares in Ephesians 5:33 to be the basic blueprint for a good marriage: *"Nevertheless let every one of you in particular so **love his wife** even as himself; and the wife see that she **reverence her husband**."* From the same chapter, Paul defines what true love for one's wife includes: stable leadership (vv. 22-24), sacrificial service (v. 25), sanctifying ministry (vv. 26-27), satisfying needs (vv. 28-30), and security (v. 30). The wife is to respect her husband's authority (his God-given position over her) and submit to His leadership, as he submits unto the Lord.

Truly, Isaac and Rebekah's marriage was a match made in heaven. Some patriarchs took more than one wife, usually for the wrong reasons, but Isaac had eyes only for Rebekah and never took any other woman as his wife. What a splendid picture of the love the Lord possesses for the Church for all eternity.

Apparently, Isaac and Rebekah enjoyed 98 years of good married life together, but then something happened which would affect their relationship forever. Esau and Jacob, twins, were their only children; Esau was the older. The marital hardship began when Isaac sought to pass the birthright blessing unto Esau, his favorite son.

During this time, recognizing important events and solemn occasions with a feast was customary. The passing on of the family birthright constituted such an occasion, so Isaac charged Esau to prepare a feast and then proceeded to dictate the menu—savory venison, his favorite food. This is a sad commentary on Isaac—he allowed his own appetite to delay the important spiritual matter at hand. This same propensity for self-indulgence has crippled many families in our present culture. Fathers are occupied with satisfying their own base appetites with temporal things rather than with the important spiritual matters of raising godly seed, while mothers are labouring outside the home only to find that their mobility exposes their minds to secular propaganda, undue stress, and disquieted children who feel undervalued. The mighty dollar has no value in heaven unless it is spiritually transformed here and now for the glory of God and the furtherance of His kingdom (Luke 16:9). Let us not squander what has spiritual significance for that which is for fleeting gain with no eternal value.

The Lord had told Rebekah before her sons were born that her younger son, Jacob, would rule over her older son, Esau

(Gen. 25:23). From her point of view, God needed some assistance in restraining Isaac from conferring the birthright blessing to Esau. After all, it was God's will—right? She knew the blessing did not belong to Esau, so she was determined that he would not receive it, despite undermining her husband's authority in the family. This pattern of events and the resulting consequences in the marriage of Isaac and Rebekah is all too prevalent in Christian marriages today.

This downward spiral of family harmony begins when the husband does not love his wife sacrificially and does not guide his family with good spiritual leadership. Then, the wife, who normally submits to her husband's authority as unto the Lord, responds to his poor leadership with the unscriptural behaviour of manipulation. The flesh, however, has never been successful in controlling the flesh, so the problem only worsens. At first, her controlling techniques are subtle, and she is almost unconscious of her attempts to move her husband to a higher plain of spirituality. Subsequently, as time squanders by, manipulation is perfected, and a deep-seated controlling pattern evolves. If not corrected, in time these techniques will become so refined and inherent within the marriage relationship that they are accepted as the norm. The consequence—healthy, intimate communication is lost in the relationship. Disclosure and intimacy will never be fostered in a relationship as long as one spouse is trying to control the other.

This pattern of control is exactly what happened to Isaac and Rebekah's marriage. Isaac lost Rebekah's heart in Genesis 26 when he had passed her off as his sister. Thus, in Genesis 27, when Rebekah did not see Isaac doing God's will—not doing what she knew of God's will—she took matters into her own hands, directing Jacob, now a grown man of some 77 years of age, to lie and deceive his elderly father. Jacob knew better. Note Rebekah's commands to Jacob in verses 8, 13, 43, and 45:

"obey my voice" and *"I will send and fetch thee."* God's order in the family collapsed that day, for Jacob obeyed his mother's deceptive instructions, and the family reaped the consequent chaos.

Another factor in this tragedy for the family was that the parents had favorites among the children. Esau was Isaac's favorite son, and Jacob was Rebekah's (Gen. 25:28; 27:5-6). All children are a gift from God and should be loved and treated accordingly; parents should be good stewards of such blessings (Ps. 127).

A natural propensity of our nature is to impose our will upon others, to try to control or manipulate each other. Whether directed at friends, our spouse, family members, or church brethren, these tendencies will lead to broken communication and hard feelings. The following is a list of "Dirty Fighting Strategies for Getting Your Own Way" from David Augsburger's book *When Caring is Not Enough*.[1] Review these selfish bents, and if the Lord speaks to your conscience, repent, and forsake the behaviour.

1. **Timing**—Catch them off guard rather than choose a good time.
2. **Turf**—Pick your best turf rather than choose a neutral place.
3. **Anxiety**—Step up anxiety rather than set a caring atmosphere.
4. **Fogging**—Filibuster, fog, and fume instead of communicating equally.
5. **Mystifying**—Ramble, chain react, confuse rather than be clear and honest.
6. **Generalizing**—Universalize and exaggerate instead of simplify and focus.
7. **Analyze**—Intellectualize, theorize, advise instead of admitting pain.

8. **Gunnysacking**—Save up grievances rather than deal with here and now.
9. **Neutrality**—Be silent, superior, detached rather than open and present.
10. **Temper**—Hide anger, then ventilate rage rather than clean anger.
11. **Blaming**—Find who is at fault rather than practice no-fault fights.
12. **Righteousness**—Find who is right instead of find what's right.
13. **Exit**—Walk out, clam up, shut off instead of working through.
14. **Questioning**—Use clever or concealed questions instead of statements.
15. **Triangling**—Pit people against people instead of dealing firsthand.
16. **Put-downs**—Use sarcasm, jibes, digs rather than share humour.
17. **Undermining**—Undermine self-esteem rather than enrich self-respect.
18. **Guilt**—Play either judge or martyr to hook guilt not responsibility.
19. **Mind-reading**—Read or rape the other's mind rather than listen, wait, learn.
20. **Delaying**—Ignore, forget, postpone rather than honour commitments.

Rebekah usurped Isaac's authority and blatantly deceived her husband; consequently, her manipulation would result in a major family ruckus. For the scheme to work, Jacob was compelled to lie more. Only by lying and deception would his father be bamboozled. Jacob listened to his conniving mother's direction, and together they conned old and nearly blind Isaac out of issuing Esau the birthright blessing.

Throughout this chapter, Isaac's carnality was met with Rebekah's carnality—flesh against flesh. Was there any question what the result of this matter would be? One sin leads to another if not confessed, and the personal consequences in this family piled up rapidly. Others may not detect our sin, but it will always find us out: *"Be sure your sin will find you out"* *(Num. 32:23).* It may expose itself through a plagued conscience, emotional disorders, or physical pain, etc., but unconfessed sin will eventually find us out—it is a promise. Rebekah was in the process of learning this lesson. Isaac agreed with Rebekah's concern about Jacob finding a wife and sent him away to Haran. Rebekah's strategy was simple; after Esau had calmed down, she planned to send for Jacob and fetch him from Paddan-aram (Gen. 27:45). Her deceitfulness and manipulation would have a high price, however. She would never lay eyes on her beloved Jacob again. This family would be adversely changed forever.

The lesson for husbands is simply to love your wives selflessly and be good spiritual leaders. If you pursue these two ministries in your marriage, your wife will most likely not resort to nagging or manipulation to get you to do what you really know you ought to do anyway.

What do you think Rebekah would have done if she could have relived that day? I think, knowing the full cost of her actions, she would have submitted to her husband's rule over her and trusted God to work out the details in His timing. Even when the situation doesn't make any sense, leave the matter with the Lord. Ladies, if your husband is spiritually lethargic, surrender him unto God, but **do not** try to impose your will upon him through manipulation. Solomon has a good bit to say about the wife who resorts to these tactics:

A foolish son is the ruin of his father, and the contentions of a wife are a continual dripping. —Proverbs 19:13 NKJV

It is better to dwell in a corner of the housetop, than with a brawling woman in a wide house. —Proverbs 21:9

It is better to dwell in the wilderness, than with a contentious and an angry woman. —Proverbs 21:19

It is better to dwell in the corner of the housetop, than with a brawling woman and in a wide house. —Proverbs 25:24

Everyone is under some human authority, and Paul informs us that when we oppose that authority we are opposing the counsels of God (Rom. 13:1-2). Unless, of course, the lower authority contradicts God's authority, in which case we should passively reject such authority and willingly suffer the consequences patiently (Acts 5:29-41; 1 Pet. 2:19-20). God has imposed human authority over us for the purpose of teaching us to submit to Himself. Trying to control, defame, or taint the authority God has placed over us is an insult to His order and His authority.

Men that are constantly ridiculed, diminished, and, consequently controlled by their wives don't achieve stature or honour in the eyes of their children. In the end they usually become spiritual washouts in the home and in the church. A husband locked into this nagging and belittling existence soon will have no motivation to think for himself: "Why bother making a decision—it won't be right anyway." "She always finds something to be critical about." Matrimony of this sort is nothing less than torture. The husband seemingly only has two escapes from the lashing tongue: he can either docilely settle into lowly servitude and abject aversion or run. Neither avenue of evasion will benefit the family. In the former, the husband lives with his wife, but not for her, and in the latter, he does neither. Wives, encourage your husbands in spiritual leadership, but don't nag! Rather, compliment him when he does what is right. If you cannot say anything kind to your husband, then be silent for "waters that babble, in their course proclaim their shallowness, while, in their strength, deep streams flow silently." Provoke him unto love and good works through your godly, quiet conduct. Extend genuine love to him, regardless of whether he demonstrates love to you or not.

> *Love is patient, love is kind. It does not envy, it does not boast, it is not proud. It is not rude, it is not self-seeking, it is not easily angered, **it keeps no record of wrongs**. Love does not delight in evil but rejoices with the truth. It always protects, always trusts, always hopes, always perseveres.*
> *—1 Corinthians 13:4-7 NIV*

True love releases hurt into the Lord's care, keeps no record of wrongs, is not selfish or proud, and seeks the good of the other spouse. The willingness to release wrongdoing (Eph. 4:32) and to pledge forgiveness when sins are confessed (Luke 13:3) is evidence of Christian love within the believer. *"And above all things have fervent charity [love] among yourselves: for charity [love] shall cover the multitude of sins" (1 Pet. 4:8).* "Tell us some of the blunders your wife has made," a radio quizmaster asked a contestant. "I can't remember any," the man replied. "Oh, surely you can remember something!" the announcer said. "No, I really can't," said the contestant. "I love my wife very much, and I just don't remember things like that."[2] There is absolutely no room for rage, resentment, revenge, or bitterness in marriage. These attitudes are foreign to God's desire for marital companionship and only cause division and loss of blessing within the marriage and family life.

If you love, you will suffer, and if you do not love, you do not know the meaning of a Christian life.

—Agatha Christie

What's at stake if husbands and wives do not pursue God's design for a healthy marriage? The erring marital behaviour of Isaac and Rebekah negatively affected the next generation. The consequences of a dysfunctional marriage clearly carry over into future generations. When husbands do not sacrificially love their wives and lead the home with a spiritual mindset, the whole family suffers. Habits are learned and, unfortunately, passed down to the children. A nagging, degrading wife not only affects her husband, but her children, future grandchildren, and saints in the local assembly. She also suffers, for her husband never reaches his full potential in the Lord. He fails to fulfill the family and church roles he was chosen by God to perform. Therefore, ladies, pray for your husbands, encourage them and respect them, but do not try to control, nag or belittle them, especially in front of others. Do not engage in the profession Charles Dickens so colorfully described as "henpeckery."

Not his shame nor his scorn,
But a virtuous wife I'll be,
Not rot of bone to mourn
But a solace framed in purity.

Selfish ambition I shall shed
That others may note and see
The shining crown upon his head
Which is the light of Christ in me.

—W. A. Henderson

59

The Vine

The Clinging Vine

Thy wife shall be as a fruitful vine by the sides of thine house... —Psalm 128:3

"What a year for tomatoes!" I exclaimed to my children while plucking another ripe tomato from an outspread row of prolific vines. While admiring the appealing fruit and no less appreciating the abundant harvest, the extraordinary word picture of Psalm 128:3 came to mind, *"Thy wife shall be as a fruitful vine by the sides of thine house."* It is divine parallelism with far reaching significance. In what manner is a virtuous wife like a fruitful vine?

In ancient times, fruit-bearing vines were commonly planted adjacent to the exterior walls of homes. Practically speaking, the custom optimized ground space, provided protection for the vine, and allowed easy access to the delicious fruit. From a cosmetic sense, cold barren walls were transformed into radiant color, for the fruitful vine was an ornament of beauty. Yet, neither the bountiful fruit nor the adorning aspects of the vine developed naturally—a labour of love was necessary to achieve both. To become fruitful, the fragile vine required a ***place*** to be nurtured, a ***purpose*** to guide development and specific ***provisions*** to ensure fruit-bearing.

The Place of the Vine

The vine clung to the side of the house. Paul instructed both Timothy and Titus not to leave this important detail out in providing pastoral direction to God's people. To Titus he wrote, wives should be *"discreet, chaste, keepers <u>at home</u>, good, obedient to their own husbands, that the word of God be not blasphemed" (Tit. 2:5).* The Greek word in many manuscripts that is translated "keepers at home" in this verse is *oikouros* (oy-koo-ros'). *Oikos* means "home" and *ouros* refers to "a guard;" thus, the keeper at home is literally the "guardian at home."

To Timothy, a warning was attached to the instruction given in Titus 2:5, *"that the younger women ... **guide the house** [sphere of delegated responsibility], *give no occasion to the adversary to speak reproachfully" (1 Tim. 5:14).* Concerning this warning Warren Wiersbe writes:

> "Guide the house" (1 Tim. 5:14) literally means "rule the house." The wife should manage the affairs of the household, and her husband should trust her to do so (Prov. 31:10-31). Of course, marriage is a partnership; but each partner has a special sphere of responsibility. Few men can do in a home what a woman can do. Whenever my wife was ill, or caring for our babies, and I had to manage some of the affairs of the home, I discovered quickly that I was out of my sphere of ministry!

> The result of all this is a good testimony that silences the accusers. Satan (the adversary) is always alert to an opportunity to invade and destroy a Christian home. The word *occasion* is a military term that means "a base of operations." A Christian wife who is not doing her job at home gives Satan a beachhead for his operations, and the results are tragic. While there are times when a Christian wife and mother may

have to work outside the home, it must not destroy her ministry in the home.[1]

Satan eyes the disordered home as an opportunity to gain an *occasion* and promote further chaos within the family. Disorder leads to frustration and often an atmosphere of resentment, then ill temper invades family life. Now entrenched, Satan continues to assault the family from the very strongholds we have allowed to become permanent in our minds (2 Cor. 10:4-5). A good mother will both guard against the evil that is craving to invade her home and endeavour to keep an ordered home within which evil does not arise. In so doing, she minimizes Satan's opportunity to wreak havoc upon her family. He is not so much interested in the family itself, but in defying God's order and marring an earthly manifestation of submission to divine authority.

Where will the vine yield her best fruit? If the fruitful vine spreads her rich foliage about the floor of the home, she certainly will be trampled upon and damaged. If she were to spring up and adhere to the roof top, she might seek dominion over the home, and her fruit would be lofty and inaccessible. The best possible place for the vine to be planted and cultivated is alongside the home. God designed the woman, the fruitful vine, for unique fruit-bearing. He created marriage and ordered the home with this purpose in mind. The vine will not thrive upon the floor or the roof; God did not create the woman for man to wipe his feet upon nor was she created to rule over him. From man's side, she was drawn, and by man's side, she shall instinctively endeavour to reside. Her natural place to cling is at home and at her husband's side. This is God's best plan for woman.

Wives, if you want to rattle your husband's demeanour a bit, occasionally whisper softly in his ear, "I am your clinging vine." What you are declaring to him is that you are yielded to God's order for *your* home and that you are settled in *your* divinely-appointed role. With God's help and His Word to guide, you are declaring that you want to be marvelously fruitful at home!

The Purpose of the Vine

The vine was profitable; it bore delicious fruit. The vine was attractive, pleasing to gaze upon. One of the greatest delights of Christian fellowship is to be refreshed in a home managed by a godly woman. The work of the Holy Spirit is evident in her peaceful countenance, her selfless hospitality, and her discreet behaviour. The vine's plentiful, easily-imparted fruit ensures an atmosphere of leisure and comfort for her guests to enjoy.

> There is no spectacle on earth more appealing than that of a beautiful woman in the act of cooking dinner for someone she loves.
> —Thomas Wolfe

If such a woman has children, a double blessing to her houseguests is obtained from the fruit of her womb. *"Lo, children are an heritage from the Lord: and the fruit of the womb is His reward" (Ps. 127:3). "Correct thy son, and he shall **give thee rest**; yea, he shall give **delight unto thy soul**" (Prov. 29:17).* Well-mannered, self-sacrificing and respectful children are a rich blessing to any guest in the home. However, selfish, disobedient and unruly children torment visitors.

I recollect being in the home of a young Christian couple during a pastoral call. Inside the walls of this home dwelt two of the most skillful wee sinners I had ever beheld (one boy and one girl). The toddlers didn't pay the bills, write out the grocery list or even carry out the garbage, but they virtually controlled the household. These stubby delinquents were well-dressed and clean, but outrageously disobedient and unrestrained—metaphorically speaking, well-garnished, but decisively rotten fruit. The mental anguish to the parents and to myself was exhausting as boisterous chattering, temper tantrums and back-talking repeatedly interrupted our conversation. Children left to their own foolishness will disgrace their parents and descend into their own self-seeking agenda. Untrained and undisciplined children will simply display the natural law that is within their hearts. *"The heart is deceitful above all things, and desperately wicked: who can know it" (Jer. 17:9)?*

One of God's primary purposes for marriage is revealed in Malachi 2:15: God desires a "godly seed." Not just numerous children, as commonly taught by some, but "godly children."

> The commonest fallacy among women is that simply having children makes one a mother—which is as absurd as believing that having a piano makes one a musician.
>
> —Sydney J. Harris

Ideally, mothers spend the most time with their children and, thus, have the most mentoring and nurturing opportunities. The goal is to develop godly children who will be a blessing to others. But how is this accomplished? *"The rod and reproof give wisdom; but a child left to himself bringeth his mother to shame" (Prov. 29:15). "Foolishness is bound in the heart of a child; but the rod of correction shall drive it far from him" (Prov. 22:15). "A foolish son is the heaviness of his mother" (Prov. 10:1).* It doesn't matter if we are speaking of your fools or mine—children are naturally foolish. If not corrected, a fool will act foolishly. To put it concisely and to avoid drifting too far into the matter of child-training at this juncture, children must be trained not to remain fools. Teaching, encouragement, mentoring, challenging, rebuking, and punishing children for disobedience are all involved in training children for the Lord. Mothers have a simple choice of either "train" or "shame"!

> The most important occupation on earth for a woman is to be a real mother to her children. It does not have much glory to it; there is a lot of grit and grime. But there is no greater place of ministry, position, or power than that of a mother.
>
> —Phil Whisenhunt

Provisions for the Vine

The vine is a weak and tender plant, which requires both "support" to adhere to the side of the house and "direction" to guide the growth where it is desired. In God's plan for the home, the wife is to be the nourisher, and the husband is to be the supporter (provider). The husband is to care for the wife as he would a fragile and delicate vase (1 Pet. 3:7). It becomes essential that the husband provide a good balance of both tender support to his wife (which includes encouragement and sacrificial love) and direction (spiritual leadership) for her to follow. If the vine does not receive adequate support, the winds of adversity may break and cast the vine down to the ground. Discouragement and depression will follow, and the loveliness and fruitfulness of the vine are abruptly lost.

Likewise, if the vine is not directed properly in growth, it will follow its own way. A vine may turn towards the roof (assume authority in the family), or laterally reach some obscure location (engage in activities unprofitable for the family), or perhaps extend downwards into base living, only to be trodden under the foot of corruption. In any case, an unguided and unattended vine will grow in such a way that good fruit-bearing is diminished or lost altogether.

Husbandry in ancient times meant "labouring in agriculture." Biblically speaking, this is exactly what God demands of husbands throughout time—to be husbandmen. These are real men, who will nurture, support, and guide their wives so that they may be thriving fruitful vines that adorn their homes. Remember gents, an ideal wife is any woman who has an ideal husband! If your wife is not the woman you think she ought to be, first ask yourself if you are the man God wants you to be. The answer is invariably no. God made woman in such a way that, if she discerns genuine, sacrificial love and solid, spiritual leadership from her husband, she will, generally speaking, follow the intrinsic programming God implanted deep within her being from the beginning.

> Be to her virtues very kind;
> Be to her faults a little blind.

> —Matthew Prior

The vine requires both emotional support and spiritual direction from her caretaker to be fruitful. When all of her needs are satisfied, the vine will provide delightful refreshment. If the husband is demonstrating a sacrificial, obligatory type of love to his wife (not to be confused with pity), she will naturally, if relying on God's transforming energy and wherewithal, bear fruit. If the husband is abiding in the Lord Jesus, he will skillfully prune, guide, and support his vine to ensure fruitfulness. But, if the husband fails to pursue Christ as his first love, he will doubtlessly neglect his vine and the clamouring of his flesh will be a clumsy substitute for master husbandry.

The Fruitful Vine

We conclude with one last glimpse of the elegant vine clinging to the house by which the Sovereign planted it. The vine has lavishly spread her beautiful foliage over the entire wall. "How was this accomplished?" someone asks. It is because her attentive husband has carefully directed her growth and ensured that every shoot and branch is properly upheld and supported. Her prolific, luscious fruit is captivating and the envy of all onlookers. Those fortunate enough to enjoy her abundance are refreshed and sent forth with a song in their hearts and the praise of God on their lips.

Clusters of the Vine

*This thy stature is like to a palm tree, and thy breasts to clusters of grapes. I said, I will go up to the palm tree, I will take hold of the boughs thereof: now also thy breasts shall be as **clusters of the vine.** —Song of Solomon 7:7-8*

One man acquired more practical experience in relationships with women than perhaps any other married man in human history. Through marital union, King Solomon joined himself to 1000 women (1 Kgs. 11:3). Because he sought *"an understanding heart to judge the people" (1 Kgs. 3:9)* instead of riches, power, or an extended life, God rewarded him with immense wisdom. Unfortunately, wisdom is often overpowered by lusting, and in the latter years of his monarchy, his foreign wives lured his heart away from following the Lord (1 Kgs. 11:2).

Solomon was a prolific writer. His literary handiwork was 3000 proverbs and 1005 songs (1 Kgs. 4:32). Yet, one song, *The Song of Solomon*, stood out from among all the others. Solomon called it *"The song of songs" (Song 1:1)*. Interposed with this literary masterpiece is Solomon's wisdom, his apparent remorse for polygamy, and the most romantic interlude of a husband and wife in all Scripture. In this song, he upholds God's best for marriage—one man and one woman becoming one until death parts them, (and God's best in marriage) and exhilarating companionship.

The Song of Solomon is a marital opus of devotion and commitment between a husband and his Shulamite bride. Although several interpretations and viewpoints are extended for this song, the one I believe to be the most fitting is the literal explanation of King Solomon and a young Shulamite woman being mutually consenting lovers who maintained moral purity in their relationship until they were married.

If indeed the "beloved" is Solomon, the typology of a Jewish King obtaining a peasant Gentile bride unmistakably represents the mysterious relationship of Christ and His Church. The Shulamite maiden in this song is initially black (sun-baked) and comely (unworthy), but after being joined to her Jewish groom, he proclaims to her, *"thou art all fair, my love; there is no spot in thee," (Song 4:7)* which is staggeringly familiar to Paul's teaching concerning the Church and her relationship to Christ. Initially, we were ungodly and enemies of God (Rom. 5:6, 10), but through our union with Christ, we have been reconciled with God and accredited a position of righteousness (Rom. 4:5). Even now, Christ continues to sanctify and cleanse His bride, and in a future day, He will present her to Himself without spot or wrinkle (Eph. 5:26-27).

The young maiden was swept off her feet during her first encounter with Solomon. Perhaps, he had disguised himself and ventured from the palace secretly to enjoy a few moments of solitude in the countryside. Her family was jealous of her infatuation with the King and at the remote possibility that she could live in the palace, have a life of luxury, and have preeminence over them. To ensure that she would be less available for fanciful consorting, they forced her to work grueling days in a vineyard. Solomon sensed this family situation and returned to the one he admired disguised as a shepherd. Like Christ, Solomon laid aside his royal apparel and glory to become a lowly shepherd in order to commune with his love.

The Shulamite insisted that Solomon not gaze upon her in her adversity, but for him, her subjection to her family authority just made her more desirable. He responded to her plea by saying, *"Thou art fairest among women."* The glorious king had returned to commune with his lowly bride and to snatch her away to live with him in the palace, which sounds incredibly similiar to the blessed hope of the Church. The Lord Jesus said to His disciples the night before He was crucified, *"In My Father's house are many mansions: if it were not so, I would have told you. I go to prepare a place for you. And if I go and prepare a place for you, I will come again, and receive you unto Myself; that where I am, there ye may be also" (John 14:2-3).*

Putting the mysterious typology of Song of Songs aside, reviewing the spectacular interaction of these two lovers would be valuable in determining what is both meaningful and edifying conduct within our own marriages. The Song of Solomon contains many lessons in how both husbands and wives may satisfy one another's needs for companionship.

They Had Doves' Eyes For Each Other

The bridegroom proclaims of his bride, *"Thou hast doves' eyes" (Song 1:15; 4:1).* The bride speaks of her beloved as having *"eyes like the eyes of doves" (Song 5:12).* As C. E. Hocking comments in his book, *Rise Up My Love*:

> The dove spoken of here is the 'rock pigeon,' which hides away from danger among the stony crevices of a rock face. Normally, like eyes, these doves are always seen in pairs. Both lovers describe the others' eyes as doves' eyes. Indeed, her eyes are a true mirror image of his and his eyes of hers. …Beauty and constancy are suggested, for the dove has its

mate alone before its eyes, and mourns when its mate is absent.[1]

The husband and wife literally have eyes only for each other. Recently, my wife and I strolled hand in hand along a beach that gently inclined as it vanished into the Pacific Ocean. From a distance, I noticed that we were nearing some sparsely-dressed women basking in the sun. As we neared them, I determined to gaze upon the beauty of God's natural creation instead of His self-flaunting creatures. After we had walked past these women, my wife, who had been between the sunbathers and myself, affectionately seized by arm in hers and said "Thanks." Turning to peer into her gleaming face, I replied "For what?" Her response was simple, "For having eyes for me." Men, your wives notice those quick glances at forbidden fruit, and each one of them bruises your fruitful vine and limits the ascent to true biblical companionship. Do you want your wife's affection or anxiety?

As Paul notes, the traditions of men have often imposed the unjust restrictions of *"touch not; taste not; handle not" (Col. 2:21)* upon our liberty. But, it is good to remember that the naïve young man of Proverbs 7 was brought down into sin by a strange woman who appealed to all five of his senses. Might we add, "look not," "listen not," and "smell not" to this list as a guide for husbands to follow concerning inappropriate sensual behaviour with other women. Having doves' eyes for each other is a much deeper realm of commitment. A husband and wife who have doves' eyes for each other will long to be with each other and a deep sense of yearning will be felt when they are apart for very long.

Furthermore, doves cannot rotate their eyes to see; they must turn their necks to look in different directions. Their fixed eyes convey single-hearted devotion to one another. Having doves' eyes for one another necessitates being with one another. A husband and wife must spend time together to nurture their relationship. Except for rare unavoidable excursions or when the "provider" role of the husband removes him temporarily from his wife's presence, husbands and wives should generally adopt the motto, "Where you go, I go, and where I go, you go." Let the shadows of you and your spouse not part for very long!

Husbands and wives should endeavour to have a mutual vision and mission in the home and a common ministry to those outside the home. In other words, they should choose activities they can do as one, serving God together. It may not always be possible for one to minister in the same way as the other, but in spirit and in prayer, they should never part. Husbands and wives are to have "doves' eyes" for one another.

He Accommodates Her Moods

Medically speaking, women in childbearing years have three powerful hormones constantly changing on a monthly cycle. These hormonal fluctuations affect a woman's disposition and mood. The natural effect of these hormones varies among women. For some women, the result will be more physical in outcome, while others will struggle with depression, anxiety, and irritability. Husbands should first thank the Lord that they don't have to endure the hormonal changes that their wives do (though they have their own hormones to deal with). Secondly, husbands should be sensitive to their wives' mood changes and assist them as much as possible. Hocking highlights the way the beloved accommodated his bride's needs in the first poem (Song 1:2-2:7):

> The whole poem appears to oscillate between the country and the city, the vineyards and the banqueting house, the

sovereign and the shepherd. She needs to be conducted from one scene to the other so as to assure her heart, for she is overly self-conscious. This her beloved does with great sensitivity, responding to her initial request to him 'Draw me', and so accommodating himself to her every mood until she is faint with love and finally requests 'stay (support) ye me'. The experienced attractions, responses, and triumphs over all obstacles, led to the attained rest of betrothal.

We may note that she:

is drawn by him	is sustained by him
is brought into the king's chambers	is brought to the banqueting house
desires his kisses	enjoys his embrace

There is development elsewhere in the poem:

she suffers from sun scorching	then she is under his shadow
she is slaving away in the vineyards	she is sitting down in his presence
we will run after thee	love is not to be disturbed[2]

Just as Christ satisfies every need of the Church, husbands should endeavour to satisfy every legitimate need of their wives. A properly satisfied wife will respond to her husband in the same way the Shulamite woman responded to Solomon—with total commitment and returned affections. God created woman to respond in this way upon the receipt of genuine sacrificial love.

Her Preoccupation with Self

Mark the Shulamite girl's preoccupation with herself in this poem (She uses the pronoun "I" eight times compared to Solomon's single use.). She is especially sensitive to her appearance. In contrast, Solomon focuses the majority of his speech (three of the five verses) on reassuring the Shulamite of his love and on approving of her beauty.

In general, women are more concerned about their outward presentation than men. Men may venture from the home into public without inspecting their appearance, but to do this would be unsettling for most women. Socializing prior to gazing into a mirror and sprucing up a bit? No way.

Both Paul and Peter address the feminine practice of alluring with the outward (1 Tim. 2:9, 1 Pet. 3:3). The woman's long hair is referred to as her glory (1 Cor. 11:15), and evidently even Christian women were displaying their hair in elaborate columns of braids. They were flaunting themselves in costly apparel and decorative ornaments of gold and fine jewels. In short, these sisters in the Lord were highly embellished stumbling blocks for the brethren. They were flirtatious and misusing their feminine assets to attract the attention of their male counterparts. Nothing is new under the sun, but time has shown that this enticing practice continues to degrade women and stumble men. With each passing generation, women are uncovering more of themselves; consequently, sexual perversion abounds.

Returning to the Song of Solomon, the exhortation is twofold.

Men: Understand the natural need for a woman to be noticed and appreciated, then continually reassure your wife that she is the "apple of your eye." She needs to know that you only have doves' eyes for her. The husband in the Song of Solomon ministered to his wife in this way: *"Thou art fairest among women," "Thou art all fair, my love; there is no spot in thee," "As the lily among thorns, so is my love among the daughters."* Truly, a husband with such tender qualities casts a *"banner of love"* over his wife (Song 2:4).

Women: A woman has no scriptural grounds to be a seductress. A wife should endeavour to look her best for her husband in the home, but why would you desire to be more highly decorated in public? Who would you be trying to impress? Certainly not the Lord! Clement of Alexandria summarizes this point bluntly, "Love of display is not for a lady, but a prostitute".[3] Show love to the brethren by not stumbling them in their thought-life. Choose to cover up instead of make up!

She Spoke Kindly of Her Husband

The Shulamite is swelling with kind speech about her beloved, but she spends more time *talking about him* to others than speaking *to him*. The Shulamite never says anything negative about her beloved to others. There is no excuse to talk disrespectfully or disgracefully about your husband to anyone else; *"the wife see that she reverence her husband" (Eph. 5:33).* One of the deepest needs of men is to feel respected by their wives. It is possible that a wife may spell submission with a capital S but still taint her husband's authority through verbal disrespect of him while speaking to others. The army has an old saying—"salute the uniform not the man." Your husband may not have earned your respect, but you still must respect his position of authority, for it was issued by God. If you disrespect his authority, you oppose God (Rom. 13:1-2).

If you have an issue with your husband, discuss it with him alone, but don't demean him with slander or gossip. If the matter cannot be resolved, seek confidential counseling. A wife who speaks ill of her husband to others sins against the Lord and her husband, for he is God's authority in the marriage. Her gossip will only serve to hinder open communication and true companionship within the marriage for she will be blotting out the positive by focusing her mind on the negative and her husband's basic need to be respected will clearly be unmet.

She was Reserved for Him Only

Obviously, not everyone who passes by the home can pluck off whatever fruit from the vine he or she desires, or there would be diminished beauty to adorn the home, reduced provision for the family, and less consolation for the husband. Certainly, the wife's generosity must be balanced by the priorities previously stated. She must deliberately withhold part of herself from being expended in the daily routine in order to be able to refresh her husband. She should be consciously saving back a provision of her strength and emotional reserve to minister to her husband's needs.

Speaking of his wife, Solomon expresses this provision of refreshment eloquently:

> *This thy stature is like to a palm tree, and thy breasts to clusters of grapes. I said, I will go up to the palm tree, I will take hold of the boughs thereof: now also thy breasts shall be as **clusters of the vine**, and the smell of thy nose like apples; and the roof of thy mouth **like the best wine** (Song 7:7-9).*

The metaphoric language is quite powerful in the above passage. To alleviate confusion, we will call upon C. E. Hocking to simplify and clarify the similes and symbols:

> For her beloved, too, her breasts are as clusters of fruit. By means of this simile he is not describing their youthful and graceful beauty, but *rather their maturity and abundant fruitfulness*. Like dates, her fruit was sweet and nutritious *to his soul*. Every impression she makes upon him creates deep desires within him, so that he determines to make her his own.

> Note his repeated "I will.".... It remains for him to appeal to
> her: she must become all that he desires her to be.... It is not
> the vine in budding and flowering stages that He seeks, but
> He would handle and taste its abundant fruitfulness. Hence
> his desire that her "breasts be as the clusters of the vine.[4]

The Shulamite was offering Solomon her best—fine clusters of grapes (mature, selfless, and abundant love) from her one vineyard (her own body, Song 8:12)—her best wine (prepared love to please his senses). Wine in the good sense symbolizes joy in Scripture, *"wine that maketh glad the heart of man" (Ps. 104:15)*. Christ joyfully anticipated drinking wine with His disciples in the coming kingdom (Luke 22:18). Foresight and preparation are required for a wife to be able to joyfully give her best to satisfy her husband's need for affection. It took hard work to produce wine, and it cost the grapes everything (we speak of mature love that longs to satisfy). Some work is necessary for the wife to have something left to present to her husband in those few minutes of the day remaining after the children are occupied with sleep.

Each woman is different. For some, it may mean taking time for a short nap in the afternoon in order to get "charged up" a bit for the evening hours. For others, it may mean exercising to become more emotionally alert and physically energized. Some women (the non-nappers) may just start the day a bit later in order to obtain sufficient sleep to maintain the physical stamina needed for the day's agenda. Whatever works for you, be consistent so that you have some vigor left to share with your husband. The clusters of grapes were visibly fresh, tantalizing to taste, and thoroughly satisfying. Do your best, and try not to serve "leftovers" too often.

Turning to husbands for a moment, let us apply the vine and grape imagery. Drunkenness is consistently forbidden throughout Scripture. Paul exhorts believers "*be not drunk with wine, wherein is excess; but be filled with the Spirit" (Eph. 5:18)*. In moderation, the fruit of the vine may stir up joy, but if abused, it certainly will control our flesh. This is also true of your fruitful vine at home. The vine expends much energy to bear clusters of grapes. The fruit requires time to develop and ripen; it is simply not available at all times. Likewise, the husband should be careful not to be too demanding of his vine; moderation will ensure satisfying refreshment from the vine, but excess will certainly affect the quality of fruit and the general health of the vine.

It is quite possible that the Mosaic law pertaining to the feminine menstruation period was invoked to protect a woman from being abused by her husband, for a man was not allowed to touch his wife during that time and for an entire week afterwards. In application, Warren Wiersbe finds this to the spiritual principle that may be invoked in our present day.

> Certainly God created sex for pleasure as well as for procreation, but pleasure that isn't disciplined soon becomes bondage and then torture. Unmarried people must exercise self-control lest they commit fornication and invite the judgment of God (Heb. 13:4), but married people also need self-control lest they take advantage of one another and leave God out of their most intimate relationship.[5]

God created sex, but indulging any craving of our flesh beyond moderation will tend to derail us spiritually. The romantic side of marriage should be balanced, and men, your tender vine is to be cherished, nurtured, and not abused.

A second note of application for husbands is this: A good husbandman attends to his vine first, then enjoys its fine fruit later. In romantic interaction, this principle is certainly a good one to follow.

Thirdly, the husband's sexual needs are to be satisfied only by his wife. God consecrated marriage for such ministry, which absolutely ensures that there is no room for immorality, pornography, phone or internet sex, or any lascivious behaviour. Wives, keep your husbands accountable, and do not tolerate **any** such behaviour. Every image he views will ultimately be compared with you. Satan then has the opportunity to stir up dissatisfaction and entice a lusting thought-life. Let us call it what it is—sin! It is totally unfair and unrealistic to compare the finest looking 18-year-old model with your wife who has aged because of time and exhausting service, and who has borne you several children. Get real guys; grip reality, and don't make a provision for your flesh!

> *Drink waters out of **thine own** cistern, and running waters out of **thine own** well. Let thy fountains be dispersed abroad, and rivers of waters in the streets. Let them be **only thine own**, and not strangers' with thee. Let thy fountain be blessed: and rejoice with the wife of thy youth. Let her be as the loving hind and pleasant roe; **let her breasts satisfy thee** at all times; and be thou ravished always **with her love.***
> *—Proverbs 5:15-19*

> *Nevertheless, to avoid fornication, let every man have his **own wife**, and let every woman have her own husband. Let the husband render unto the wife due benevolence: and likewise also the wife unto the husband. The wife hath not power of her own body, but the husband: and likewise also the husband hath not power of his own body, but the wife. Defraud ye not one the other, except it be with consent for a time, that ye may give yourselves to fasting and prayer; and come together again, that Satan tempt you not for your incontinency.*
> *—1 Corinthians 7:2-5*

Whether she is spoken of metaphorically or in plain language, a man is to have his own wife and none other. Let him enjoy his own vine, his own cistern, his own well—his own wife! On this matter of marrital fidelity, Matthew Henry writes:

> Let him then scorn the offer of forbidden pleasures when he is *always ravished with the love* of a faithful virtuous wife; let him consider what an absurdity it will be for him to be *ravished with a strange woman (Prov. 5:20)*, to be in love with a filthy harlot, and *embrace the bosom of a stranger*, which, if he had any sense of honour or virtue, he would loathe the thoughts of. "Why wilt thou be so [stupefied], such an enemy to thyself, as to prefer puddle-water, and that poisoned too and stolen, before pure living waters out of thy own well?"[6]

Solomon provides wonderful insights within the Song of Solomon as to the appropriate and needful interaction between a husband and his wife. Let us pursue what is holy, meaningful and edifying to our spouses, and may every husband be satisfied by the clusters of his own vine and the refreshing drink from his own well!

The Flourishing Vine

I went down into the garden of nuts to see the fruits of the valley, and to see whether <u>the vine flourished</u>, and the pomegranates budded. —Song of Solomon 6:11

Come, my beloved, let us go forth into the field; let us lodge in the villages. Let us get up early to the vineyards; let us see if <u>the vine flourish</u>, whether the tender grape appear, and the pomegranates bud forth: there will I give thee my loves. —Song of Solomon 7:11-12

The Shulamite bride and Solomon shared a private but exhilarating and exciting romance. Both the husband and the wife actively communicated with words their passion for each other. Their free speech demonstrates the security and integrity of their love for one another. The Hebrew poetry is both lovely and pure! King James quotations in this section are from the Scofield Study Bible to ensure the reader understands some archaic expressions in their natural context.

The following are passionate expressions of the bride towards her beloved:
Let him kiss me with the kisses of his mouth (Song 1:2).
A bundle of myrrh is my well-beloved unto me, he shall lie
    all night between my breasts (Song 1:13).
Our bed is green (Song 1:16).

I am sick with love (Song 2:5).
Thy lips, O my spouse, drop like the honeycomb; honey and milk are under thy tongue (Song 4:11).
I am my beloved's and my beloved is mine (Song 6:3).
I am my beloved's, and his desire is toward me (Song 7:10).
Let us get up early to the vineyards ... there will I give thee my loves (Song 7:12).
Many waters cannot quench love, neither can the floods drown it (Song 8:7).

Solomon's passion is equally emphatic:

Rise up, my love, my fair one, and come away (Song 2:10).
Thy hair is as a flock of goats, that appear from Mount Gilead (Song 4:1).
Thy lips are like a thread of scarlet (Song 4:3).
Thy neck is like the tower of David builded for an armory (Song 4:4).
Thy two breasts are like two young roes that are twins, which feed among the lilies. Until the day break, and the shadows flee away, I will go up to the mountain of myrrh and to the hill of frankincense (Song 4:5-6).
Thou art beautiful, O my love (Song 6:4).
How fair and how pleasant art thou, O love, for delights (Song 7:6)!
This thy stature is like to a palm tree, and thy breasts to clusters of grapes. I said, I will go up to the palm tree, I will take hold of its boughs; now also thy breasts shall be like clusters of the vine; and the fragrances of thy breath, like apples, and the roof of thy mouth, like the best wine (Song 7:7-9).
Set me as a seal upon thine heart, as a seal upon thine arm; for love is strong as death (Song 8:6).

If you are not familiar with the Song of Solomon, you may have been surprised or even stunned by the fervent poetic dialogue between these two lovers. In biblical days, a Jewish man was not permitted to read this text until he was 30 years old. Some might have even felt a bit embarrassed with the graphic references of disclosed affection. If so, we must remember that we are reading the inspired Word of God! The unfettered passionate interlude of a husband and wife is one facet of companionship that God designed for us to enjoy. There is nothing shameful in a husband and wife intimately divulging their hearts to one another.

When the bride speaks of her beloved resting all night between her breasts (or upon her bosom), she is poetically speaking of her longing for sweet uninterrupted communion with her husband. Unfortunately, our western culture has tarnished our thinking, and some may have envisioned some X-rated scene being depicted. This is not the case! The sexual aspects of these lovers are completely veiled in secrecy and rightly so. Their mutual love for each other and enjoyed communion, however, is highlighted in Scripture.

An important lesson can be learned about what might be revealed and what should be concealed in a marriage relationship. Details about the physical exchange between a husband and wife should remain concealed from others, unless counseling is sought in this area (a decision which must be mutually made). However, the outshining glow of two people in close enthusiastic communion with one another cannot be concealed even if the couple tries. How did Abimelech know that Isaac and Rebekah were married? He noticed Isaac caressing Rebekah (Gen. 26:8). Even this pagan king understood the marital language of a man to his wife, and as a result, their deception was found out.

Although obligational love (commitment) holds the marriage together, disclosure builds intimacy, and shared passion imparts joy to the union. The romantic side of a marriage is just one way to share passion and build intimacy. However, we are creatures of habit and rote. If a couple is not attentive to one another, they may sail their marriage into the doldrums of stagnated romance. Keep exploring new avenues of romancing one another—like you did when you were first married!

Husbands, drop your wife a brief note in the mail, or hide a romantic poem, so she will find it during the day. Take a moment here and there just to embrace and hold her and to reaffirm that she is the only love of your life. Schedule "get aways" without the children at least once or twice a year. Try to set aside one night a week just to spend time with your wife (you don't necessarily need to go out and spend money, just put the kids to bed early). Taking frequent walks together allows time to communicate, to appreciate God's creation, and to clear from the mind a bit of the daily routine. Be innovative, and keep your love fresh.

Wives, men are generally stimulated by their senses, notably by sight. In Proverbs 7, Solomon warned his son of the destructive force of a strange woman upon a young man destitute of knowledge. As mentioned earlier, her seductive assault battered all five of his senses. With his flesh stirred up to lusting, he cast all reason into the wind and yielded to her urging: *"He goeth after her straightway, as an ox goeth to the slaughter" (Prov. 7:22).* He would rather die than think! Outside of marriage, the sexual sin of the woman is to lure and of the man is to follow. Within the marriage, *"the bed* [is] *undefiled" (Heb. 13:4).* Practically speaking, ladies, you may have to sacrifice that long flannel nightgown for a "spicier" substitute once in a while. Try using music, candles, sensual gestures and the like to arouse your husband. Experiment, have fun! Don't ever get stagnant with this aspect of your marriage.

The Shulamite bride did not have much to offer Solomon, other than her own vineyard (metaphorically speaking, her own body). At first, her time attending to the grape vineyards distressed her, for it was difficult to properly care for her own body while working strenuous hours in the hot sun. *"**Look not upon me**, because I am black, because the sun hath looked upon me: my mother's children were angry with me; they made me the keeper of the vineyards; but **mine own vineyard have I not kept**" (Song 1:6).* But once in the palace, she was able to attend to her own vineyard (body) as she proclaimed, *"my very own vineyard is at my disposal" (Song 8:12, NASB).* This was a choice she made: to take good care of herself, then to wholly give herself to her husband. Wives, attend to your own vineyard, then seek to satisfy your husband with the sensuous fruits of the flourishing vine.

As people grow older, they change in different ways. Solomon colorfully describes the condition of those in their autumn years: *"In the day when the keepers of the house shall tremble, and the strong men shall bow themselves, and the grinders cease because they are few, and those that look out of the windows be darkened" (Eccl. 12:3).* It is natural for older women to fall, for men to slump over with age, and for the elderly to lose their teeth and eyesight—the outward perishes. Likewise, the avenues of exchanging marital passion with each other will also change with age. Enjoy the changes, and seek to develop new expressions of mutual pleasure. So, go exploring, and enjoy each other within the natural realm that God has given.

Perhaps the greatest blessing in marriage is that it lasts so long. The years, like the varying interests of each year, combine to buttress and enrich each other. Out of many shared years, one life. In a series of temporary relationships, one misses the ripening, gathering, harvesting joys, the deep, hard-won truths of marriage.

—Richard C. Cabot

The disclosure between husband and wife must remain pure, private and undefiled by frivolous exposure to others. God sternly warns against forsaking physical intimacy in a marriage: *"Marriage is honorable in all, and the bed undefiled: but whoremongers* [fornicators] *and adulterers God will judge" (Heb. 13:4).* The marriage act is a gift in itself to be shared between a husband and his wife. However, the emotional entanglement and soul meshing that occurs when two people pour themselves into one another during physical bonding is much more consequential than the fading moments of physical arousal. The sense of pleasing one's spouse surmounts the goal of mutual satisfaction.

The world teaches to love self, to please self, and to deal with your throbbing conscience and guilt later. Is this what God teaches? Listen to Paul's words written to the church at Philippi about how to have joy in relationships with others:

> *Therefore if there is any consolation in Christ, if any comfort of love, if any fellowship of the Spirit, if any affection and mercy, fulfill my joy by being like-minded, having the same love, being of one accord, of one mind.* **Let nothing** *be done through selfish ambition or conceit, but in lowliness of mind let each esteem others better than himself. Let each of you look out not only for his own interests, but also for the interests of others. Let this mind be in you which was also in Christ Jesus. —Philippians 2:1-5 NKJV*

The only way for a husband and wife to be like-minded is to have the mind of Christ. The Lord Jesus always attended to the needs of others first. In this way, He demonstrated true love all the way to the cross. Likewise, a spouse must have the mindset of pleasing one's partner first to experience the full thrill that God intended for their interaction. The goal of this physical rendezvous is mutual satisfaction, but an unselfish attitude of giving is the only means to accomplish this goal. Those who engage in intimate activities outside of marriage will never experience the full emotional intimacy the marriage act was designed to promote because no commitment is present between the parties to allow for full disclosure! In an elementary sense, it would be like eating a Big Mac without being able to taste or smell it. The visual sense confirms you're eating it, but you have no satisfaction in partaking of it!

The Hebrews 13:4 verse application, in my opinion, extends far past the bedroom. Certainly, God is warning husbands and wives not to forsake the wholesome physical bonding within a marriage for another outside the marriage. However, God often uses adultery to describe the spiritual, emotional, and physical defilement of His people with idols, materialism, and worldliness in general.

James 4:4 contains a strong exhortation to Christians in this regard: *"Ye adulterers and adulteresses, know ye not that the friendship of the world is enmity with God? Whosoever therefore will be a friend of the world is the enemy of God."* James is not talking here about physical adultery but spiritual adultery—replacing our intimacy and devotion to God with irrelevant things and secular relationships. This type of adultery is a common thread woven through the entire Old Testament as Israel, the wife of Jehovah, frequently commits spiritual adultery against God and is finally divorced and judged until the ultimate restoration of a Jewish remnant occurs during the tribulation period (Jer. 3:8; Ezek. 16:15-38; 36:16-25; Hos. 2:23).

Likewise, some confidential emotional aspects of marriage are more far-reaching than sexual expression. These intimate revelations of companionship should be kept consecrated and treasured within the boundaries of matrimony. Husbands and wives should nurture this unique oasis of disclosure and post a "No Trespassing" sign at the perimeter of this private domain.

Then as often as possible, they should sneak away and visit their privately created realm of exposure, enjoyment and ecstasy.

Motherhood

The Joyful Mother

*He maketh the barren woman to keep house, and to **be
a joyful mother** of children. Praise ye the Lord.*
—Psalm 113:9

Not only did God create woman for motherhood, but motherhood was created for woman. When will a woman experience
the most joy and satisfaction in life? When she submits her will
to the Lord's will and aligns her thinking with the mind of
Christ. Thus doing, she then intently pursues God's plan for her
life. It is understood that some women are contemplating marriage, but are waiting in singleness, while others have been
called to singleness. However, either case allows women to better serve the Lord unhindered by family responsibilities (1 Cor.
7:34).

The bountiful harvest of souls within foreign lands during
the last two centuries is due in part to the service of single
women missionaries. In the late nineteenth century, Hudson
Taylor was criticized for sending teams of unmarried women
into the interior of China as missionaries (a situation created by
the lack of single men responding to his invitation to evangelize
China). In the twentieth century many Christian organizations
were reporting unmarried women missionaries were outnum-
bering single men by a ratio of 8 to 1. The CMML *2002 Missionary Prayer Handbook* indicates single missionary women
outnumber single missionary men by a factor of 4.4 to 1.[1]

TEAM reported a ratio of 4:1 in 1999 and of the 2,000 active missionaries (including short-termers) with SIM, 75 percent are married and nearly all of the remaining 25 percent are women.[2] Praise the Lord for all those sisters who have sacrificed personal aspirations to further the kingdom of God. Such servants derive joy in pleasing the Lord apart from marriage and motherhood.

It is also understood that some married women are unable to have children. These women have the opportunity to serve the Lord in some unique and special capacity without the burden of caring for a family (unless, of course, they care for children through adoption or foster care). But if we examine the oracles of God with unpretending reverence, we clearly behold motherhood as God's grand plan for woman. She was created in God's infinite wisdom and predetermined counsel to fulfill this ministry. She will, thus, derive the most joy in life by aligning her thinking and pursuits after sovereign counsel.

In the general sense, the desire to conceive, bear and nurture children is a deep-seated and essential need of the woman. These instinctive maternal yearnings were designed by God to ensure population growth and the proper care of children. Furthermore, the Spirit of God specifically records the mental anguish of many wives who could not bear children to ensure that we recognize both His plan for woman and her need to adhere to His design. Barren Sarah begged her husband Abraham, *"go in unto my maid; it may be that I may obtain children by her"* *(Gen. 16:2)*. A wife who pleads with her husband to lay with another woman is certainly desperate for children. When *"Rachel saw that she bare Jacob no children, Rachel envied her sister; and said unto Jacob, 'Give me children, or else I die'"* *(Gen. 30:1)*. Rachel's plight was so overwhelming that she would have rather died than remain childless. Hannah *"was in bitterness of soul, and prayed unto the Lord, and wept"* over her barren state (1 Sam. 1:10). Zacharias and Elisabeth, an older couple with no children, were granted a miraculous conception, and Elisabeth bore John, the forerunner of the Lord Jesus. Elisabeth's declaration of praise clearly indicates the emotional distress she had endured for years: *"thus hath the Lord dealt with me in the days wherein He looked on me, to take away **my reproach among men**" (Luke 1:25).*

Sophocles concisely epitomized the woman's need: "Children are the anchors that hold a mother to life." A woman who has surrendered to her maternal calling will wholeheartedly agree with May R. Coker: "Motherhood is the greatest privilege of life."

The Lord understands the home's need for children. Doctor Luke wonderfully emphasizes the humanity of our Lord Jesus in his Gospel. Only Luke records the Lord's compassion for parents who had lost all their children. The Lord raised the widow of Nain's **only son** from the dead (Luke 7:12). On another occasion, He raised Jairus' daughter from the dead; she was his **only daughter** (Luke 8:42). The Lord also healed a demon possessed boy who was his father's **only child** (Luke 9:38-40). God implanted a strong inherent desire for children into the woman, and He understands the great loss when children are absent from the home.

Paul lobs a promise into the hands of every mother willing to lay hold of it and run: *"She shall be saved in childbearing" (1 Tim. 2:15).* How does childbearing save (deliver) a mother? Home-focused mothers experience a deliverance, a salvation in a sense, from the jeopardy of the world. Purity is not robbed from the wife's mind by raging gossip, evil conversations, and lewd exhibitions. Secular stresses and professional pressures are never invoked, and her exposure to temptations is minimized.

Secondly, it saves her from the loss of reward at the Judgment Seat of Christ. The primary calling of the woman and, thus, the most general way she will impact the kingdom of God is by marrying a husband, and by bearing and nurturing godly children. Susanna Wesley, though not a perfect woman, understood her divine calling. If she had been less dedicated to her home or to rearing spiritual children for God, our hymnals would be divested of hundreds of entries and tens of thousands of lost souls would have continued on their downward plunge into the horrors of hell.

Unfortunately, many Christian mothers are presently pursuing selfish ventures rather than cleaving to God's revealed plan of motherhood. In doing so, they squander the opportunity to please God and to reserve for themselves a greater reward in heaven. Rewards received at the Judgment Seat of Christ are a direct measure of the believer's ability to worship God in glory and of the appreciation of heaven that he or she will have throughout eternity. Glory has a weight to it (2 Cor. 4:17), and after glorification, some believers will shine brighter than others (1 Cor. 15:41-42). *"She shall be saved in childbearing"* ensures that a mother will find the most joy, satisfaction in life, and heavenly reward, not by ascending the corporate ladder, but by fulfilling her God-ordained role as nurturer.

The author is not advocating the chaining of mothers to the kitchen table or the imprisoning of them within domestic quarters. Simply stated, every time a mother ventures away from the safety of her home, there is a greater possibility of exposure to evil. The home is a safe haven where she can thrive while fulfilling her divine calling without secular distraction. Think of how many extramarital relationships would have been avoided if wives had engaged in the Lord's work in their homes rather than in seeking man's filthy lucre through secular employment or in trying to satisfy a craving for prestige and power through a professional career!

While writing this portion of the book you hold, the author received a telephone call from a struggling single mom with four children. This young woman, a new Christian, intensely wants to please the Lord, but her situation constantly forces her to choose between the "provider" and the "nurturer" roles in her family. She confessed that she is not doing well in performing either and daily witnesses the consequences of a one-parent family in the training of her children. Emotional exhaustion and self-imposed guilt overshadow her daily routine. Her words to-day expressed one of the deepest longings implanted in women by the Creator: "I need a husband to take care of this kind of stuff and me too, so I can be free to raise my children for the Lord." She was not saying that God was incapable of being a Father to the fatherless or that He was unable to relieve the widow (Ps. 146:9), but that family life outside God's best design was prone to frustration and consequences. Moms need dads, and dads need moms in unique and diverse ways!

A mother in the home has a strong influence upon the way her children view their father. Children esteem their father to the extent that their mother esteems him. If mom instills excitement in the children when dad returns home at the end of a workday, the children will then be filled with jubilation when they first see his face. Mothers should endeavour to accentuate the positive characteristics of their husbands and their role as family leader before the children and render criticism privately far away from little ears. James Dobson writes: "A mother plays a vital role as the primary interpreter of a father's personality, character, and integrity to their children. She can either help them bond together in love, or she can become a wedge that keeps them apart."[3]

Dads should follow the same practice. One should not engage in airing marital difficulties, arguments, or insults in front of your children. A single volley of harsh words may taint their pliable and impressionable minds for life. Husbands and wives must edify one another, especially in the presence of their children. A practical example would be that when one of your children acknowledges a tasty meal, mom perhaps could respond, "I just cooked what your dad laboured for and what God provided." Dad could perhaps respond, "Your mom can make anything taste good."

Submitting to divine roles in the home does not demean women or exalt men—it glorifies God. God created woman with intelligence, creativity, and a merciful insight into people—qualities that fit her for success in many professions. Yet for her to succeed in the professional realm, she must first turn her attention, at least in part, from the one career for which those virtues were dispensed—motherhood! Moms cannot do both well. Many women who engage in both secular employment and motherhood are running ragged; some trudge through life in a constant state of fatigue and exhaustion. Many have tried the part-time professional approach, but the children invariably see a part-time mom. This statement may be offensive to some, but it is simply God's truth.

Unfortunately, many mothers have been compelled to find employment because of family financial woes. It is understood that overwhelming circumstances may necessitate a mother having to work outside the home for a brief period of time. It is understood that poor financial choices prior to salvation impose lasting consequences. But in God's best plan for the family, moms were not to be providers and nurturers—God did not design woman to do both! It is my opinion that, during financial distresses, the head of the family, the provider, should seek to secure extra work before asking his wife to depart from the higher priority home ministry to engage in secular employment (i.e. to take a second job).

Why is God's foremost design for the family not being taught in many of our local churches? Invariably because esteemed teachers or prominent individuals in authority have wives who work outside the home and delegate the care of their children to others. Who will love and serve a child the best? A substitute caretaker who is receiving pay to attend to many children at once, or the child's natural mother? Church leaders should be setting a good example, but instead, many undermine God's best for family-life. God is not mocked, and ultimately, their accountability will be with the Lord!

> I am a woman, not a man,
> > created second in God's plan.
> To find what role in life I play,
> > I read God's Word every day.
> I find content that I must be
> > to let a man rule over me;
> This does not mean that in this life,
> > I'm unimportant as a wife.
> My husband needs me by his side.
> > To be his "helpmeet," I take pride.
> As a mother, I gladly share
> > my time, my love, and tender care.
> So many tasks are mine to give,
> > they're never finished while I live.
> God's plan for womanhood is good;
> > I wouldn't change it if I could.

> —Lois Patterson

The Virtuous Woman

When one considers all that the "virtuous woman" of Proverbs 31 accomplishes, she might better be recognized as a present-day "wonderwoman"—a make believe super-hero. The word translated as "virtuous" in verse 10 of that chapter is derived from the Hebrew word *"chayil."* In this application, the word paints the portrait of a wholesome, industrious, efficient, profoundly able wife. Let us gaze a bit more closely at this incredible example of femininity.

In verse 11, we read that *"the heart of her husband doth safely trust in her."* Verse 12 continues with *"she will do him good, and not evil all the days of her life."* This wife has won her husband's full confidence. She is the ultimate selfless companion who longs to serve her husband instead of placing expectations on him. Verses 12-19 describe a woman who rises early in the morning to greet the day with hard work. Matthew Henry clarifies the virtuous wife's mindset: "She doesn't love her bed too much in the morning."[1] The virtuous woman puts forth her best efforts in keeping the home and pleasing her husband. She is industrious and frugal. Neglect and ease are not words in her vocabulary.

How might we depict a modern day Proverbs 31 woman? Well, such blessings come in all sorts of different shapes, sizes, and agendas, but most are easy to spot! The portrait of one such virtuous heroine would be something like this. Her mini-van proudly displays the bumper sticker *"Caution: Driver Brakes for Garage Sales."* She is frugal and finds the best prices for her family's needs whether it is at the supermarket, dry cleaners, or her best friend's garage sale. She tends a garden to ensure the freshest vegetables for her family's consumption and preserves an ample supply for winter use. Through rigorous mending and repair work, she ensures safe passage of all her children's clothing from origination "awesome" to designation "outgrown." She greets the cashier in the checkout line with a cheerful "Good morning" while, at the same time, handing over a fist full of crumpled coupons. She may be recognized as the woman who serves nutritious meals throughout the day, orchestrates the homeschooling of her children, pulls off both a shopping trip and the kids' piano lessons in one afternoon, executes a fly-by house cleaning just prior to serving dinner, and still can greet her honey with a smile when he arrives home. Truly, a Proverbs 31 super-hero!

Although the Proverbs 31 woman is industrious *in the home* and loyal to her husband, she is also compassionate. Verse 20 proclaims, *"she stretcheth out her hand to the poor; yea, she reacheth forth her hands to the needy."* What a legacy to leave to her children. *"He that giveth unto the poor shall not lack: but he that hideth his eyes shall have many a curse" (Prov. 28:27).*

This virtuous woman understands that *"every beast of the forest is Mine* [God's], *and the cattle upon a thousand hills ... for the world is Mine, and all the fullness thereof" (Ps. 50:10-12)* and that her *"children are an heritage of the Lord: and the fruit of the womb is His reward" (Ps. 127:3).* What she has is really not hers but God's. She has merely been entrusted with temporal wealth and eternal souls (her children)—a serious stewardship. Therefore, she *"casts her bread upon the waters" (Eccl. 11:1)* knowing that the Lord pays wonderful dividends on what is loaned to Him, which is really His anyway. She gives often and willingly, knowing that everything that is bestowed on the needy is given unto the Lord and to the praise of His name.

One of the finest legacies a mother can impart to her children is an unselfish example. Children will pattern themselves after a recurring exhibition of selflessness. This elegant aspect of "motherhood" was well displayed following one evening meal in our home.

The whole family (five of us at this juncture) was still seated around the dining room table and engaging in idle chitchat, when my bride announced, "There is a package of honey buns on the counter if anyone wants dessert!" An immediate radioactive glow emanated from three juvenile dessert addicts as they rose up a bit in their chairs. My daughter promptly spun out of her chair and dashed to the kitchen counter. She brought an opened box of "honey buns" back to the table and, after completing a few algebraic equations, formulated a startling conclusion, which she announced to the group, "There are only four honey buns in this box, but there are five people." Before these words had scarcely escaped her lips, her mother piped in with, "That's OK guys I don't want one."

A momentary pause hung over the table, as everyone pondered her sincerely selfless act, the like of which has often garnished our home. Another sibling broke the silence, "We can cut them up, so we can all have some." My son was now pursuing the example just witnessed. Mom, however, didn't indulge her sweet tooth that night, and consequently, four honey buns met their doom through lethal ingestion. The arousal of our palates was vanquished in a moment, but beyond the realms of distinguishable sight and sound, a fragrant pillar of selflessness gently floated upward as sweet incense into the very nostrils of Almighty God.

A noticeable outshining of the Lord Jesus can be seen in every believer when the prompting of the Holy Spirit to offer some aspect of self is obeyed. These living sacrifices capture the luster of the risen Saviour, subsequently bringing refreshment to the heart of God!

Practically speaking, moms can encourage children to give of themselves in many ways. Visit your local nursing home, retirement centre, rescue mission, or hospital on occasions. Perhaps, the children could even grow vegetables for the local rescue mission or others in need. A care package of homemade goodies and colored pictures or crafted gifts from the children will resurrect long forgotten smiles upon the faces of those in the autumn years of their lives. Yes, your children may have to endure a pinch on the cheek or nursing home odours, but they will learn early in life the joy of sacrificing themselves for the good of others. Also, don't forget those suffering loneliness during the holiday season or at other times.

This past year, ten children (from the ages of 3 to 8) arrived on our front porch one frigid December evening to sing several Christmas carols and to share memorized verses about the Christmas story. It was a special thrill to see the smiling faces of children sharing the "reason for the season." The remainder of the evening was delightful, as the whole family cherished the little bouquet of joy that had been gently bestowed upon the threshold of our hearts. In the same way, a plate full of goodies and a cheerful smile will be instrumental in not only cheering up your lonely neighbors but perhaps in witnessing to them also. If you have older children, maybe a widow who lives nearby needs her house painted, windows washed, leaves raked or the lawn mowed. They could also assist younger mothers by offering a few hours of childcare or house cleaning services. One must simply open one's eyes to behold a vast sea of hurting, lonely, and needy people. Help your children to open their eyes and to develop compassionate hearts as well.

As a mother leads her children in ministry, the home becomes an outpost of heaven. Children must be exposed to, told about, and experience the glorious things the Lord is doing in our lives. *"Let Thy work appear unto Thy servants, and Thy glory unto their children" (Ps. 90:16).* The main sphere of this revelation of glory will be in the home, so seize every opportunity to share with your children, your excitement for God, your vision for ministry, and how the Lord shows His glory through your service and prayer life. In this way, your children will eagerly expect God to deal with them on the same personal level. This will truly affect our children for eternity. John Phillips commenting on Psalm 90:16 writes:

> God is intensely interested in our children. We need to see God's mighty arm bare in their lives. We need to pray that He will do His work in them. They need to see His glory for themselves. Let us plead for a fresh expression of the might of God, for a work pointed by God directly into the hearts of our children and young people.[2]

•Verse 23 of Proverbs chapter 31 is paramount: *"Her husband is known in the gates, when he sitteth among the elders of the land."* The gate of the city was the common location for business and the seat of government. The gate was the strategic location for any politician as he could shake hands with everyone who entered the city. Why could the husband be devoted to his business at the city gate? Because he had a wife who was totally devoted to her business at home. He was not concerned about the daily activities of the home. This sphere of responsibility was delegated to his wife in whom he had the utmost confidence.

The practical and wise instruction of this woman to her children is captured in verse 26: *"She openeth her mouth with wisdom; and in her tongue is the law of kindness."* She is not prone to speaking evil of others or spreading gossip about them. Her tongue is a skillfully-controlled instrument of instruction, edification, and healing. Solomon recognized the awesome power of the tongue, *"death and life are in the power of the tongue" (Prov. 18:21),* and the virtuous woman is profoundly "pro-life."

The mother is the one who establishes the tone of response in her children. If she is prone to be quick to anger and unforgiving, her children, likewise, will tend to be easily enraged and bear a yoke of bitterness (application from Prov. 22:24). If mom speaks foolishly, the children will follow in her folly (application from Prov. 13:20). It is well said, *"Whoso keepeth his mouth and his tongue keepeth his soul from troubles" (Prov. 21:23).*

The mother's heart is the child's schoolroom.

—Henry Ward Beecher

The virtuous mother will seek to instill virtue within her children through the instruction of God's Word. The Apostle Paul reminded young Timothy of this motherly responsibility: *"When I call to remembrance the unfeigned faith that is in thee, which dwelt first in thy grandmother Lois, and thy mother Eunice; and I am persuaded that in thee also" (2 Tim. 1:5).* Why could Timothy have unshakable faith? Paul answers this question a bit later in the same epistle: *"But continue thou in the things which thou hast learned and hast been assured of, knowing of whom thou hast learned them; and that from a child thou hast known the holy Scriptures, which are able to make thee wise unto salvation through faith which is in Christ Jesus"* *(2 Tim. 3:14-15).* Timothy had a mother who toiled in laying a solid footing of Scripture to pour his foundation of faith upon. From his "formed" faith, he would properly judge his emotions and be a wise master builder.

Dear believer, never get this important construction project upside down! The *fact* of Scripture leads to derived *faith*, which serves to discern and judge our *feelings*. If a Christian allows his or her feelings to define their faith, invariably the Word of God will be interpreted by mood and circumstance! Our feelings cannot be trusted, for they are prone to constant change, but God's Word is immutable and trustworthy.

Parents are exhorted to instruct their children from God's Word throughout the day: *"These words, which I command thee this day, shall be in thine heart: and thou shalt teach them diligently unto thy children, and shalt talk of them when thou sittest in thine house, and when thou walkest by the way, and when thou liest down, and when thou risest up" (Deut. 6:6-7).* One advantage of homeschooling is that parents are afforded more time with their children and, therefore, can apply life's naturally-occurring teachable moments as object lessons. Mothers have the unique opportunity to mold our future.

The woman who creates and sustains a home and under whose hands children grow up to be strong and pure men and women is a creator second only to God.

—Helen Maria Fiske Hunt Jackson

The hand that rocks the cradle is the hand that rules the world.

—William Ross Wallace

Proverbs 31:30 reads *"Favour is deceitful, and beauty is vain: but a woman that feareth the Lord, she shall be praised."* Our industrious mom doesn't worry about the natural degradation of aging. She realizes that the body is just a temporary shell, a container of what is real and eternal. Unwarranted concerns about facial wrinkles, gray hair, and sagging tissue fall into the realm of vanity.

Several years ago, I was in a checkout line in a local hardware store. After my purchases had been tallied, I handed the cashier, a woman in her early twenties, a credit card to pay for the merchandise. My wallet was lying open on the counter, and while I waited for the return of my credit card, the cashier canvassed a picture of my family in the top foldout. She remarked, "What a nice family, and what a pretty wife you have." My response moved her to tears: "If you knew my wife, you would understand that she is far more beautiful than pretty." Nearly every aspect of our society measures and markets the worth of a woman by how God has wrapped her instead of the contents of the inner person. This standard is contrary to the teaching of Proverbs 31 and the rest of Scripture.

Proverbs 31 concludes with a phenomenal tribute to "the virtuous woman." In verse 28, she receives the praise of her children and of her husband. In verse 31, we find the grand finale: *"Give her of the fruit of her hands; and let her own works praise her in the gates."* This woman is the talk of the town and is known far and wide for her charitable, industrious, devoted nature. In today's jargon, "What an awesome mom!" Of course, in the heavenly realms, she has the praise of God, who finds her submissive, quiet and meek spirit of great value. Surely Solomon wrote of such a wondrous woman in Proverbs 18:22: *"Whoso findeth a wife findeth a good thing, and obtaineth favour of the Lord"!* It is nonetheless fitting, for the Spirit of God to uphold this virtuous woman as the crescendo of Proverbs. Sid S. Buzzell explains:

> The virtues of a noble wife are those that are extolled throughout the Book of Proverbs: hard work, wise invest- ments, good use of time, planning ahead, care for others, re- spect for one's spouse, ability to share godly values with oth- ers, wise counsel, and godly fear (worship, trust, service, obedience). As Proverbs has stated repeatedly, these are qualities that lead to honour, praise, success, personal dignity and worth, and enjoyment of life. In the face of the adulter- ess' temptations mentioned often in Proverbs, it is fitting that the book concludes by extolling a virtuous wife. Young men and others can learn from this noble woman. By fearing God, they can live wisely and righteously. *That* is the message of Proverbs.[3]

Dads are uniquely prominent in the life of a child, but there is something distinctly special about moms. Glancing back into my own childhood, it was always Mom, not Dad, that got the dandelion or assorted wild flower bouquets. It was Mom, not Dad, who would wait patiently in bed for her breakfast on Mother's Day and always acted as if the finest catering service had been provided when we finally arrived. A towel over a cookie tray, a cup of lukewarm coffee, coagulated scrambled eggs, and a petrified biscuit, however, scarcely accounted for her gratitude.

During these moments, mothers receive brief dividends on their personal investments in their children. In a flicker of time, hundreds of sleepless nights, tons of soiled diapers, thousands of baths, and a myriad of dirty dishes vanish away in the smile of one child. Yes, moms are very special people, but often we wait too long to express how much they really mean to us. The following poems are a tribute to all virtuous mothers!

I Held Her Hand

I held her hand in mine last night,
Hands so thin and worn,
And they held mine just as tight,
As the day that I was born.
Those gentle and expressive hands,
Etched by work and care,
Have folded over my bedside,
Many times in humble prayer.
They've washed me, they've fed me,
They've helped me be a man.
There's something of our Lord Himself,
In every mother's hand.
It has been said:
Youth fades, love droops, the leaves of friendship fall;
But a mother's secret love outlives them all.

—Martin Buxbaum

Only One Mother

Most of all the other beautiful things in life come by twos
and three, by dozens and hundreds. Plenty of roses, stars,
sunsets, rainbows, brothers, and sisters, aunts, and cousins,
but only one mother in the whole world.

—Kate Douglas Wiggin

The Home

Building Her House

*Every wise woman **buildeth her house**: but the foolish plucketh it down with her hands. —Proverbs 14:1*

The Hebrew word for "buildeth" is *banah*, which simply means "to build" or "to make." A wise woman builds up her home. She orders it, keeps it and makes it better. Interestingly, the first occurrence of *banah* in the Bible also relates to a woman; *"And the rib, which the Lord God had taken from man, **made He** a woman, and brought her unto the man" (Gen. 2:22).* Scripture first applies *banah* to God's creative act of fashioning woman. The second biblical usage of *banah* in relation to a woman is found in Genesis 16 where we find the barren Sarai (later named Sarah) desperately seeking children to "build up" her house.

Sarai told Abram, *"I pray thee, go in unto my maid; it may be that I may obtain children by her" (Gen. 16:2).* The Hebrew word *banah* is here translated "obtain." Sarai earnestly wanted to build up her household even if it meant her husband (later named Abraham) taking her handmaiden Hagar as a concubine. Abraham pitched tents (the dwelling place for his family) and erected altars (led his family in worship), but building the home was Sarah's job. This principle, introduced here in Genesis, is repeated throughout Scripture. In the Jewish culture, the groom was responsible for building a house prior to obtaining his bride. This was usually a modest structure near his father's home or an additional room added to father's house. Although the groom built the house for his bride, the bride was to be the builder of the household.

From the earliest pages of Scripture, we see God's plan for the family. The husband is to be the head of and the provider for his family, while the wife is to bear children, nurture them, and keep and maintain the home. In Ruth 4:11, both Leah and Rachel are acknowledged as the ones who *"did build* (banah) *the house of Israel."* Again, our theme verse reads *"Every wise woman **buildeth*** (banah) *her house, but the foolish plucketh it down with her hands" (Prov. 14:1). "Through wisdom is a house builded; and by understanding it is established" (Prov. 24:3).* The wise mother rests in God's wisdom and strength to build and to keep her home, for *"except the LORD build the house, they labour in vain that build it" (Ps. 127:1).*

The word *banah* is used 376 times in the Old Testament. Interestingly, when *banah* is associated with men, it speaks of building houses, cities, altars, the temple, etc. Examples: *"But Pharaoh's daughter came up out of the city of David unto her house which Solomon had **built** for her" (1 Kgs. 9:24). "Then Jeroboam **built** Shechem in Mount Ephraim, and dwelt therein; and went out from thence, and **built** Penuel" (1 Kgs. 12:25).* However, in each of the five times that *banah* is connected to women in the Bible, people are built up.

In general, what humankind builds rots, corrodes, degrades and, generally over time, loses value. Building a home, however, has eternal value. This observation does not diminish the father's responsibility as the spiritual leader of his family, but it does highlight the significance of a virtuous woman labouring to build up her home; her investment of time and energy literally impacts eternity!

Abraham Lincoln was strongly influenced by two spiritual women. While a mere baby, his mother was heard to say, "I would rather have him learn to read the Bible than to have him own a farm." Lincoln grew up in utter poverty and, while at a young and tender age, bore one of the hardest blows of life, the death of his mother. However, God was working in his life, and his father married another woman who was intent on little Abraham learning not only to read but to read the Bible.

Only the Creator Himself knows what contribution these two virtuous women, of humble status, had in composing the stature of the man. Later in life, while reflecting upon his own upbringing, he declared, "No man is poor who has had a godly mother."[1] Is it possible that these two women had more impact on the Civil War than any general commanding soldiers or politician governing the people at the time? It is an intriguing thought at the least and the profound reality of motherhood's power in the extreme.

A Mother's Creed

I believe in the eternal importance of the home as the fundamental
    institution of society.
I believe in the immeasurable possibilities of every boy and girl.
I believe in the imagination, the trust, the hopes and the ideals,
    which dwell in the hearts of all children.
I believe in the beauty of nature, of art, of books and of friendships.
I believe in the satisfactions of duty.
I believe in the little homely joys of everyday life.
I believe in the goodness of the great design, which lies behind our
    complex world.
I believe in the safety and peace which surrounds us all through the
    overbrooding love of God.

—Ozora Davis

The Peaceful Home

Two telltale signs quickly sum up the measure of a man in his performance as a husband and father: the countenance of his wife and the discipline of his children. A wife who is radiant and joyful and children who are well-behaved and faithful speak highly of a man. The state of a home and the demeanour of the children reflect much the same way on a woman. If the home is dirty and out of order, if the children are not organized for serving, if meals are thrown together and rarely served at the normal time, she is not "keeping the home" well. The emotional and spiritual disposition of the mother sets the tenor of the home. If mom is not happy, nobody is happy!

> Let the wife make her husband glad to come home
> and let him make her sorry to see him leave.
>
> —Martin Luther

Several inexpensive tools can be used by homemakers to maintain an ordered home: a budget, a household schedule, a job chart, and a family calendar are but a few. Several years ago, I was counseling a young man about his finances. When I asked him if he had a budget his response was "sort of." I replied, "Budgets are somewhat like salvation; you're either a 'saint' or an 'ain't'; you either have a budget or you don't."

119

Household budgets should be developed and jointly agreed upon by both the husband and the wife, then implemented by the one best equipped for managing the task, though the husband has the ultimate responsibility of ensuring the family remains solvent. If a problem with spending money unwisely on luxuries or non-essential items occurs, then a spending limit for non-necessities should be agreed upon. In other words, Jack should not buy the $1000 entertainment suite without Holly's concurrence. If one party is undisciplined, the other should then control the "cash flow" to prevent a "cash blow." The checkbook and credit card(s) should be entrusted to the responsible party to protect the family. We are not born with discipline—it must be learned.

Are you having difficulty controlling expenditures in some aspect of your family's finances? If the problem is thoughtless excursions into the wallet for non-essential expenses, try employing the "envelope method." Perhaps, you have an addiction to "fast food." Simply agree upon the amount of money you can afford to spend eating out over a month's time (perhaps include entertainment in this sum), and insert that amount of *cash* into an envelope at the beginning of each month. When the cravings for saturated fat become unbearable, simply withdraw what you require, and put back what is not used afterwards. When the envelope is empty, your cholesterol levels will subside because you will not be eating out again until the next month—unless, of course, you have some rich friends who enjoy your company! There is nothing ingenious about the envelope method; it just teaches discipline.

Why should fathers work hard as family providers? The foremost reason is to satisfy the legitimate needs of the family for shelter, clothing, and food (1 Tim. 6:8). Secondly, a brother in the Lord cannot maintain a good Christian testimony among the unsaved if he does not provide for his family (1 Tim. 5:8).

Thirdly, *"He that giveth unto the poor shall not lack but he that hideth his eyes shall have many a curse" (Prov. 28:27).* A good family budget will enable you both to live within your means and to bestow the "saved" income to others who have need. Giving your excess to those in need is a foreign concept to our stress-saturated, greedy society that earns extra to lavishly spend on lusting. But for the believer, the highroad is the low-road—*"let each esteem other better than themselves. Look not every man on his own things, but every man also on the things of others" (Phil. 2:3-4).* As discussed in the previous chapter, a notable mark of a virtuous woman is her outstretched hand to the poor and needy (Prov. 31:20). By being frugal and disci-plined to a good budget, wives immensely help their husbands in providing for their family's needs and in helping those who are in difficulty.

Most folks never realize how much money they are frivo-lously spending until they have a household budget. Budgets are not just for people who have little money to spend; budgets are for those who want to spend less money. If God has blessed you with a good income, develop a family budget in order to donate more to the poor and to the Lord's work and workers. Be a good steward of what you have been given, knowing that you shall give an account of it. Anthony Norris Groves was a wealthy dentist who left a life of luxury and comfort in the early 19th century to become a missionary to Baghdad, and then to India. He stated well what the maxim of every Christian should be, "Labour hard, consume little, give much, and all to Christ."[1] A budget will aid in this endeavour.

My home would fall into chaos without a Household Schedule, a Meal Schedule/Grocery List, a Family Job Chart and a Family Calendar. The keeper of our home (my wife) ad-ministrates all of these in one manner or another. The House-hold Schedule, which addresses all household affairs on a weekly basis, is the house-engineer's private schedule of what must be accomplished to maintain a productive and ordered home. This schedule has each day of the week listed horizontally across the top as column headings. Each of these days of the week hovers over a list of tasks, which ideally should be accomplished on the associated day. However, if a task is not completed on its assigned day, every effort will be made to complete the task the next day. If circumstances hinder a weekly task from being completed on the second day, it generally will slide until the next week, so as to preclude a snowballing effect.

The meal schedule is organized on a weekly basis to ensure a nutritional diet and that a complete grocery list can be generated to avoid more than one weekly trip to the store. Repeated trips to the grocery store adversely affect the family's budget and unnecessarily waste time. Good meal planning will promote family health, save the family time and money, and reduce frustration caused by disorder.

Household chores consist of laundry, dusting, cleaning bathrooms, vacuuming, groceries, library trips, piano lessons, gathering trash, mopping floors, schooling, washing dishes, etc. Because several hours a day are given to homeschooling our children, being scheduled becomes even more necessary. Home order will be best found in efficient routines. Normally, Mom will expend her time teaching the children in the morning, then the children will give of their time in the afternoon to help Mom maintain the home. This is practical training, as the children learn to fold clothes, wash dishes, dust furniture, cook, etc. at an early age. They will make mistakes and create messes at first, but if you keep encouraging their focused attention to the task and reiterate what is expected of them, your children will learn to be your helpers and will long to please you as well.

I cannot emphasize enough the value of starting to teach disciplined behaviour early in your child's life. None of us were born with disciplined minds or with the ability to concentrate. These aspects of fruitfulness must be learned. If parents wait to teach a work ethic until their children are nine or ten years old, or even worse, until after they are adolescents, the child will flounder in selfish ambitions. Your child might pompously conclude, "I have been served my whole life. What's in it for me to start working now?"

> The Christian home is the Master's workshop where the processes of character-molding are silently, lovingly, faithfully and successfully carried on.
>
> —Richard Monckton Milnes

Teaching children to work while they are young ensures that they will grow up being an integral part of the family. Children are aware of feeling important and valuable. It is one thing to be told that you are needed, but it is quite another to know that you are needed. Involvement in the family promotes commitment to the family! Children need to be challenged to feel significant, not vainly told that they are meaningful. I have a great concern for many young people in the present generation. In a general sense, before us presently is an over-entertained and under-challenged generation of children who are being routinely inoculated with self-esteem and New Age brainwashing. What will be the outcome? A generation of unfocused, lazy and selfish adults! It is not their fault; they have been molded to be such by a generation of tolerant, broad-minded, self-focused adults.

America's future will be determined by the home and the school. The child becomes largely what he is taught; hence we must watch what we teach, and how we live.

—Jane Addams

Another useful household tool is the Family Job Chart, which may be organized in several ways. It should be available for all to see, hanging on the family refrigerator perhaps via magnetic strips or on a kitchen wall. Many good books and charts are available on this subject. A Job Chart may be composed of a piece of paper or a dry-erase board for reusability. A possible chart, as shown below, would include four main headings—"Day of the Week," "Dishes/Kitchen Cleanup," "Weekly Jobs," "Daily Jurisdiction Areas"—then seven rows for each day of the week.

Daily Jurisdiction Areas consist of daily activities; thus, the day of the week does not apply. Under each column, write the pertinent child's name and activity as appropriate. You may either change the list after each week or at the end of the month, or you could make up four lists (or as many variations as are needed for your family) and cycle through each of them to ensure that all of the children are being challenged equally in home affairs.

The household engineer flows down task assignments to her child labour force per the Job Chart as coordinated with her overall Household Schedule. Some parents prefer to write out lists of tasks to be performed by each child during that day on a piece of paper which the child can carry with him/her while working, then mark off the task when completed. Each child is not allowed to have free time until the list has been satisfactorily completed. At first, it will be a lot of work for mom to organize the children to help her accomplish daily household tasks, but in the long run, it will lighten up her load. The children will also gain a real sense of importance within the family; they belong where they are at and are needed. To this end, they will learn to work and do so with joyful hearts.

Day of Week	Dishes/ Kitchen Cleanup	Weekly Jobs	Daily Jurisdiction Areas
Sunday	Abby/Ted		Bag Trash/Garbage - David
Monday	David/Lisa	Sweep kit. floor - Abby Laundry helper - David Kitchen helper - Ted	Bedrooms - All
Tuesday	Ted/Abby	Dust downstairs - Ted Kitchen helper - Lisa	Family Room pickup - Lisa
Wednesday	Lisa/David	Sweep kit. floor - David Dust upstairs - Abby Laundry helper - Lisa Kitchen helper - David	Get the mail - Ted
Thursday	Abby/Ted	Garbage to curbside - Ted Kitchen helper - Abby	Garden work - David/Lisa
Friday	David/Lisa	Sweep kit. floor - Ted Laundry helper - Abby Kitchen helper - Ted	Yard work - Ted/Abby
Saturday	Ted/Abby	Mop kitchen floor - Lisa Kitchen helper - Lisa Total house clean - All	Garage pickup - Ted

Lastly, the Family Calendar is important in keeping the family on target, on track and on time. Even mentioning this tool may seem like a "duh" for most families, but many still rely upon memories, scraps of scribbled-on-paper (which they can never find when needed), or someone else to remind them when and where events are happening. The family calendar organizes all of the family's planned activities by date and time.

The calendar should be large enough to write several items on an individual day, and the activity, time and place should be included on each entry. In some instances, a telephone number associated with the agenda item would be helpful in saving time from having to thumb through a telephone book to find the same number you found three weeks earlier when you made your calendar entry. If your calendar changes a lot, try using a pencil, so entries can be easily erased. The calendar should be easily accessible to the entire family (perhaps hanging on a wall in the kitchen) and near the telephone most often used.

The family budget, schedule, job chart, and calendar are all needed for household order and success. Expected family expenses are estimated and forecasted in the budget. Potential family activities are planned in an orderly manner through the calendar. The home is maintained through scheduling daily and weekly tasks to be accomplished by individuals who have received related job assignments via the Job Chart. If used properly, these four tools will establish and maintain logistical order in the home. The keeper of the home will find liberation in an ordered home. And where this freedom dwells, the testimony of a virtuous woman, which transcends human ideologies, will be sure to follow.

It has been said that there are two types of people in the world, those who *act* and those who *react*. If the keeper of the home is continually reacting to home situations instead of guiding these situations she will live a frazzled existence. When will the roller coaster ride end? Don't be a passenger; be at the helm of your home affairs. A good firefighter would much rather teach fire prevention, than respond to smoke and flames.

Titus 2:5 directs wives and mothers to be *"keepers at home."* When will a married woman experience the most fulfillment and joy in the depths of her being? Joy is composed of **J**esus, **O**thers, and **Y**ou. When a believer seeks strength and communion with the Lord to serve others, she will experience joy. The lyric to the children's song JOY by Bud Metzger reads as follows:

> Jesus and others and you,
>> What a wonderful way to spell joy!
> Jesus and others and you,
>> In the life of each girl and each boy.
> **J** is for Jesus, for He has first place,
> **O** is for others we meet face to face;
> **Y** is for you in whatever you do,
>> Put yourself third, and spell JOY!

God's blueprint of service for the wife is to be a faithful companion to her husband, to be a selfless nurturer of her children, and to be a virtuous homemaker, ensuring the home is in good working order. In so labouring, the woman ensures that her home is a peaceful oasis her husband will long for and a safe refuge her children will readily seek. Speaking to husbands, Frank Crane wrote: "Your house is your fortress in a warring world, where a woman's hand buckles on your armor in the morning and soothes your fatigue and wounds at night."[2]

The Autumn Years

Older Women at Work

While travelling down a highway or interstate undergoing road repair, eventually you will encounter a yellow sign cautioning "Men at Work." Given the *tolerant* day in which we live, I am a bit surprised that the feminists have not sued highway authorities for defamation of character and had the signs changed. Don't be surprised if, in the future, you notice a new construction sign that reads "Men and Women at Work." Of course, children might be offended that they are being discriminated against by the latter notice, so perhaps "People at Work" would be the best. But then, some lawyer, who has observed a work crew on break, will determine that the sign does not accurately represent reality, and, thus issue corrective action. The revised sign would simply read "Beware Workers in Area." Unfortunately, those suffering from paranoia won't feel safe driving any longer for fear of the construction workers. Enough satire. What we need today are older women who will buck the secular trend and labour in their God-given ministry.

If you are an "empty nester" and you have been faithful as a wife and mother, you have been commissioned by God to a teaching ministry. You cannot neglect it for there are presently too many younger women who are desperately seeking answers to questions pertaining to the home. Your counsel may give hope to a young wife in a troubled marriage; your smile may encourage the broken hearted, and your efforts in attending to the children of a new mother will allow her to obtain the rest she needs. You have amassed years of domestic experience and gained a wealth of wisdom that should be imparted instead of hoarded. Your home likely requires less of your time to keep in order now, so why not invest directly into the lives of others. Your selfless service will impact generations to come. If you have no younger women to minister to, why not extend a helping hand to the needy, or assist some Christian ministry that is furthering the cause of Christ on earth?

Paul taught an important principle about labouring for others in Ephesians 4:28: *"Let him that stole steal no more: but rather let him labour, working with his hands the thing which is good, that he may have to give to him that needeth."* God has ordered marital labouring: First, the husband labours (usually outside the home) to provide for his family's basic necessities, while his wife labours within the home accomplishing domestic duties. When this priority is met, we are not to labour more to indulge our flesh with frivolous luxuries and extravagances. These only tend to strangle the spiritual man and pull our hearts away from the Lord. No, if our necessities are satisfied we are to labour for others in legitimate need.

Because our time is important, we want to labour efficiently. When will our best proficiency be found in serving? When we apply the very skills that have already been developed in normal labouring. You would seek a plumber, not a painter, if you had a leaky pipe. The painter might be able to do the work, but it would take longer and perhaps be of lower quality. So, in application, men will labour in their normal jobs to provide extra income for those in need, while women will assist the needy with their in-home abilities or perhaps with other specific proficiencies developed by years of experience. One of the biggest travesties of 21st century church-life is that women enter the workforce after their children depart from home. Usually, the income is not even needed, but to prevent boredom, Mom seeks man's filthy lucre. Dear sisters, you have been commissioned to teach younger women essential family matters. Don't neglect this crucial ministry—it is ordained by God.

The Widow

As mentioned in a previous chapter, statistically speaking, women in the United States outlive men by approximately five years, though the gap is narrowing in recent years as more women enter the workforce. From a physiological standpoint, females mature approximately two years earlier than males, and it has been my general observation that women lead men in spiritual development also; perhaps these factors account for men generally marrying younger wives. My father is six years older than my mother and my wife's father is seven years older than her mother (they have enjoyed 62 years of marriage thus far). This age disparity was especially true in biblical days; for example, Jacob was likely Rachel's senior by some 65 years, and given the cultural ramifications of the day, Joseph was likely six to twelve years older than Mary, the mother of Jesus. Facing the mathematics of it all, women who are younger than their husbands and who live longer than their husbands will consequently encounter widowhood. If the Lord be not come, most will be widows for many years. According to Church history, the Lord's own mother braved this condition for decades.

Just as it requires time to heal a broken bone, the Lord uses time to heal the broken heart. The pain of both injuries is very real, but the healing processes are very different. Time by itself does not heal a broken heart; proper healing depends on what the grieving person does with the time. Warren Wiersbe writes:

> Each year in the United States some eight million persons experience the death of a close family member, and the loss of that loved one is very much like the loss of limb. It is an emotional amputation, and it affects you deeply. Doctors tell us that there is a definite relationship between illness and a grief badly managed. When the emotions do not heal properly, they affect the body and make the grieving person much more susceptible to certain illnesses. Loneliness and depression that are not handled in a mature way will certainly cause long-term problems that may not respond to medicine.[1]

Sin intruded into humanity with the fall of Adam; unfortunately, sorrow and death accompanied sin. But comfort is found in knowing Christ and in understanding that death only imposes a temporary separation from our loved ones in the Lord. Death is but a doorway into the presence of the Lord Jesus and into the presence of all those that He has called and will call home prior to our jubilant entrance. *"We are confident, I say, and willing rather to be absent from the body, and to be present with the Lord" (2 Cor. 5:8).* Psalm 116:15 reads *"Precious in the sight of the Lord is the death of His saints."* Why is the death of our loved ones precious to the Lord? Because, if they are believers, He is finally able to be with them in person.

It is normal to sorrow, and God has bestowed on us a capacity to grieve, to heal, and also to have hope. The Christian has a "blessed hope" despite the sorrow of death:

> *But I would not have you to be ignorant, brethren, concerning them which are asleep, **that ye sorrow not, even***

*as others which have no hope. For if we believe that Jesus
died and rose again, even so them also which sleep in Jesus
will God bring with Him. For this we say unto you by the
word of the Lord, that we which are alive and remain unto
the coming of the Lord shall not [precede] them which are
asleep. For the Lord Himself shall descend from heaven with
a shout, with the voice of the archangel, and with the trump
of God: and the dead in Christ shall rise first: Then we
which are alive and remain shall be caught up together with
them in the clouds, to meet the Lord in the air: and so shall
we ever be with the Lord. Wherefore comfort one another
with these words. —1 Thessalonians 4:13-18*

The rapture of the church is imminent and will bring all of
our suffering and sorrow to an end—*"for we shall see Him as
He is," "and so shall we ever be with the Lord."* Until then, we
must have faith that God is weaving all of our sufferings into a
broader blessing for humankind and for His greater glory (Rom.
8:28). In the interim, between His advents, we are to *"love His
appearing" (2 Tim. 4:8)* and to live in purity with holy vigor (1
Jn. 3:2-3).

Grieving for a time is natural, but it is not to overwhelm us
as one who has no hope and no God. The Lord understands our
grief, and He can identify with our sorrows, for indeed He was
the "Man of Sorrows." He wept for the grieving at the tomb of
Lazarus. It is appropriate and normal to ponder the memories of
loved ones and to grieve their "home calling," both publicly
and privately. After the death of John the Baptizer, we read that
the Lord Jesus *"departed from there by boat to a deserted place
by Himself" (Matt. 14:13 NKJV).* But after a private time of
grieving, He resumed His daily mission of serving humankind.
*"And when Jesus went out He saw a great multitude; and He
was moved with compassion for them, and healed their sick"
(Matt. 14:14 NKJV).* Those grieving should follow the Lord's

example and return to life's normal activities as soon as possible. The Lord maintained a balanced lifestyle and did not consider His return to it as being disrespectful to John.

Though private grieving is normal, it is also important to share grief and sorrow with others. The grieving individual needs to sense the assurance of personal love and the acceptance of others despite the change of marital status. The night before His suffering and death, the Lord Jesus sought comfort in the company of those who loved Him.

> *Then cometh Jesus with them unto a place called Gethsemane, and saith unto the disciples, Sit ye here, while I go and pray yonder. And **He took with Him** Peter and the two sons of Zebedee, and began to be sorrowful and very heavy. Then saith He unto them, My soul is exceeding sorrowful, even unto death: tarry ye here, and **watch with Me.** —Matthew 26:36-38*

The grieving process cannot be shortchanged, but neither should we be swallowed up by it. "Grief has its time," said Samuel Johnson. "While grief is fresh, every attempt to divert only irritates. You must wait until grief be digested."[2] Remembering that sorrow is temporary and that heaven is eternal will assist our thought-life during times of grieving.

> *Let not your heart be troubled: ye believe in God, believe also in Me. In My Father's house are many mansions: if it were not so, I would have told you. I go to prepare a place for you. And if I go and prepare a place for you, I will come again, and receive you unto Myself; that where I am, there ye may be also. —John 14:1-3*

After one has grieved appropriately and adapted to a new life of singleness, certain considerations must be pondered.

"Could I ever remarry?" "Should I remarry?" "Should I remain single to better serve the Lord?" Scripture contains several examples of women who were the heads of their homes after becoming widows. Obviously, there were many widows in biblical times who did not remarry (Acts 6:1); others, like Tamar and Abigail, did remarry. After her husband Nabal died, Abigail married King David (1 Sam. 25). Why did some widows remarry, while others did not? The main factors in this decision are the woman's age and family situation.

Abigail was a younger woman without any children. She was yet capable of bearing children (2 Sam. 3:3). Tamar's situation was similar (Gen. 38). Paul's instruction to the church is consistent with their actions: *"I will therefore that the younger women* [widows] *marry, bear children..." (1 Tim. 5:14).* Paul also states that *"she* [a widow] *is at liberty to be married to whom she will; **only in the Lord**" (1 Cor. 7:39).* In other words, the widow does not go back under her father's authority; she makes the decision to remarry or remain single herself. Her only limitation—she must marry a believing man. Abigail agreed to marry David, but her father was not involved with this decision. David chose her, and she chose David—she was not given in marriage. So, the answer to the question "Should I marry again?" is one that only the widow herself can ultimately answer, though she would be wise to seek the mind of the Lord in the unity of godly counsel. *"In the multitude of counsellors there is safety" (Prov. 11:14).*

Practically speaking, I know of one elderly widow who chose to remarry, and she simply gleams with joy and excitement. Unfortunately, I am aware of another who also remarried and has regretted the decision. No disrespect to older folks is intended, but we become more rigid in our thinking with age. We get set in our ways! Younger people are more adaptable and can more easily gravitate towards one another in their thinking, whereas older people often just dig in.

Before contemplating remarriage, the wise widow will allow sufficient time for grieving. She will seek the Lord's direction for her life through prayer, and she will seek godly counsel, determining not to render a rash decision. Satan is the high-pressure salesman; God is longsuffering and patient—wait upon the Lord. There is nothing dishonorable in a widow remarrying; marriage is clearly God's provision and protection for many widows. Elisabeth Elliot was widowed twice and remarried twice. For those who do not remarry, God Himself will attend to your needs. *"The Lord preserveth the strangers; He relieveth the fatherless and widow..." (Ps. 146:9). "Now she that is a widow indeed, and desolate, trusteth in God, and continueth in supplications and prayers night and day" (1 Tim. 5:5).*

Godly Character and Ministry

Ministry Opportunities

The contributions of women in the Bible to the welfare of others are immense, both within and beyond the realm of domestic sacrifice. Until now, we have focused most of our attention upon the general ministry that the woman was created for, namely, to be a marital companion and helper of her husband, to bear and nurture children, and to keep the home. As children mature and depart from the home, the keeper of the home will likely find that she is more available to serve others. Here are a few biblical examples of women serving the Lord.

Examples of Natural Ministry within the Home:
1. Mother Eunice and Grandmother Lois taught Timothy the Scripture from childhood (2 Tim. 3:15).
2. Jochebed received her son Moses back from the river, taught him about God, and no matter how hard those in the palace tried, they could not remove her training (Ex. 2). Moses esteemed God more than the pleasures, the wealth and the politics of Egypt (Heb. 11:24-26).
3. Hannah nursed her son Samuel and fashioned clothes for him. She journeyed to the temple and presented her son unto the Lord, as she had vowed to do (1 Sam. 1). She also prayed that his service to God would be fruitful.

4. Sarah respected her husband's authority. Her testimony serves as an example for all wives to follow: *"Sarah obeyed Abraham, calling him lord" (1 Pet. 3:6).*
5. Proverbs 31:1 reads, *"The words of King Lemuel, the prophecy that **his mother taught him**."* Lemuel's mother warned him of the dangers of embracing wayward women (v. 3) and abusing wine (vv. 4-7), and to be just and fair in all his doings (vv. 8-9).
6. The wife of Proverbs 31 was her husband's trusted companion. She was a virtuous woman, a skillful mother and a good keeper of the home—her praise was widespread.

Using the Home for Ministry:
1. Priscilla, the wife of Aquila, co-laboured with Paul in tent making and in gospel/discipleship ministry (Acts 18:2-3). It is evident from Scripture that she and her husband used their home for the kingdom of God (Acts 18:24-26; 1 Cor. 16:19; Rom. 16:5). In so doing, they both risked their lives to serve Christ (Rom. 16:3-4).
2. Martha showed hospitality to the Lord in her home (Luke 10:38; John 12:2).
3. Rahab used her home (as marked by the scarlet thread—a symbol representing the redeeming blood of Christ) to spread the warning of God's imminent judgment, and consequently, she saved a house full of people (Josh. 2, 6).
4. Peter's mother-in-law was hospitable to the Lord and His disciples (Mark 1:31).
5. The mother of Rufus was such an encouragement to Paul that he considered her his own mother (Rom. 16:13).

Serving Others Beyond the Home:
1. Joanna and Susanna provided for the Lord of their substance, likely meals and clothing (Luke 8:3).
2. Dorcas was full of good works and charitable deeds; she made garments for widows (Acts 9:36, 39).
3. Phoebe was a servant of the church, a helper of many including Paul (Rom. 16:1-2).
4. Mary worshipped the Lord by anointing His feet with precious ointment (John 12:1-7).
5. Euodia and Syntyche laboured in the gospel with Paul (Phil. 4:3).
6. Esther risked her life in coming before the king to be an intercessor for her people (Est. 4).
7. Ruth gleaned in wheat and barley fields, beat out the grain, and provided for the needs of Naomi (Ruth 2).
8. Deborah, though she did not lead the army, was a notably wise woman who rendered personal counsel to many in Israel including Barak (Judg. 4).
9. Abigail bestowed godly advice to David, and after pondering her wisdom for a moment, He replied, *"blessed is your advice and blessed are you" (1 Sam. 25:33 NKJV).*
10. Older women were and are to teach younger women how to better love their husbands and children (Tit. 2:4).

From the above examples, and others in Scripture, non-domestic ministry contributions by the sisters today would include: attendance in meetings of the church (Heb. 10:25), teaching angels about divine order and submission through the head covering (1 Cor. 11:10), financial support, prayer (1 Thess. 5:17), music (Eph. 5:19), children's ministry, mentoring other women (Tit. 2:4-5), missionary work, gospel outreach, visiting the sick, and providing clothing and food for the needy. This is by no means an exhaustive list, for our hymnals and devotional calendars all show the love of God at work through women. There is much for the sisters to do, but Scripture does provide some boundaries for their ministry also.

The Apostle Paul worked diligently to instruct and exhort the believers at Corinth concerning proper church order—they were a church in disarray. Immorality, drunkenness, worldliness, and audible chaos were the norm—as an assembly, they were not reflecting the glory of God. He taught in 1 Corinthians 11 and 14 that "church order" should reflect God's "creation order" and that visible headship should be displayed. Why? *"For God is not the author of confusion, but of peace, as in all churches of the saints" (1 Cor. 14:33).* How was God going to ensure that the church would display His glory and order? He would organize the audible and visible ministry by gender. The men, who represented the glory of God, would have their heads uncovered (1 Cor. 11:7) and would be the ones to lead and publicly speak for God in the church meetings. Not only in the New Testament but throughout the Bible, we find no example of God appointing a woman to civil, religious, or domestic authority over men. This would be inconsistent with God's creation order; something Scripture is quite clear about:

> *Let the woman learn in silence with all subjection. But I suffer not a woman to teach, nor to usurp authority over the man, but to be in silence. —1 Timothy 2:11-12*

> *Let your women keep silence in the churches: for it is not permitted unto them to speak; but they are commanded to be under obedience, as also saith the law. And if they will learn any thing, let them ask their husbands at home: for it is a shame for women to speak in the church.*
> *—1 Corinthians 14:34-35*

This is why only men were called to be apostles of the early church and why only men qualify to be church leaders (elders) of the local assembly (Tit. 1:6; 1 Tim. 3:1-2). Also, only men are to be duly appointed to the office of deacon in the local church (1 Tim. 3:11-12; Acts 6:3). However, there are some ministries reserved only for women, ministries into which men cannot intrude. The sisters, like the Kohathites of old, have been entrusted with the ministry of the coverings within the house of God. They are to cover and conceal all glories that compete with God's glory.

As the assembly gathers in the presence of the Lord Jesus, each woman who covers her head ensures that she—the glory of man (1 Cor. 11:7) and her long hair—her own personal glory (1 Cor. 11:15) are not competing with God's glory, as symbolically portrayed in the man's uncovered head (1 Cor. 11:7). This earthly activity patterns the heavenly reality where only God's glory is observed and where even the cherubim and seraphim use their wings to cover their own intrinsic glories. As Lucifer learned, God will tolerate no competing glories in His presence.

Adam and Eve also learned in the Garden of Eden that it is a strategy of Satan to lure our minds into focusing upon the negative rather than the positive. Man was invited to eat from every tree in the garden, save one. Yet, the serpent beckoned humankind to focus upon the only one off limits. What he said to the woman was essentially, "Could God be good and limit you in such an unfair way?" Satan enjoys sowing dissatisfaction, and he is still whispering the same lie into our ears today. When embraced, dissatisfaction stirs up doubts concerning God's goodness and wisdom. Doubt and distrust lead to sin and rebellion, and sin ushers in death.

The same lie which Eve believed has been modified slightly for the modern day woman, but it bewails God's unfairness and sows the same spirit of dissatisfaction. Consider the secular message of today's woman to others of their gender:[1]

> The history of all times, and of today especially, teaches that ... women will be forgotten if they forget to think about themselves.
> —Louise Otto

> Well behaved women rarely make history.
> —Laurel Thatcher Ulrich

> A free race cannot be born of slave mothers.
> —Margaret Sanger

> If divorce has increased by one thousand percent, don't blame the women's movement. Blame the obsolete sex roles on which our marriages were based.
> —Betty Friedan

Dear sisters, the next time Satan tempts you to be discontent with your God-given ministry, just remember what his rebellion accomplished for him—an eternity in hell! When temptation comes, train your eye upon all the blessings you have in Christ. Don't be tempted into thinking you deserve more than what your Creator has already graciously bestowed. You honour the Lord by abiding in His will for your life and in doing so experience the most joy in living!

The Portrait of a Godly Woman

Paul exhorted Titus to "*speak thou the things which become sound doctrine" (Tit. 2:1)* and to help others do the same, or as William MacDonald puts it, Titus' ministry was "to close the awful chasm between the lips of God's people and their lives."[1] Doctrine is more than something you learn; it is more than what is said; sound doctrine is lived! Titus was to teach God's people to live out sound doctrine by doing good works. These practical works relate to home-life, church-life, and spiritual-life in general.

Paul provided Titus with character profiles for men and women, as well as for the young and the old. The spiritual behaviour of showing love, pursuing holiness and learning to be sober-minded are clearly not gender specific; both men and women should abound in these. Beyond character itself was the visible outworking of goodness, which evidenced true spiritual vitality. What is the portrait of a spiritual woman? How is her spirituality demonstrated?

> *The aged women likewise, that they be in behaviour as becometh holiness, not false accusers, not given to much wine, teachers of good things; That they may teach the young women to be sober, to love their husbands, to love their children, To be discreet, chaste, keepers at home, good, obedient to their own husbands, that the word of God be not blasphemed. —Titus 2:3-5*

Holy in Behaviour

The Greek word *hieroprepes,* translated *"as becometh holiness,"* occurs only here in the New Testament; it means "reverent in behaviour." The Lord said, *"Be ye holy; for I am holy" (1 Pet. 1:16).* As a child of God, we are to live up to the family resemblance and to pursue holiness. This pursuit commences the moment an individual is awakened to his or her dire state of depravity, when he abandons all efforts of self-saving, repents, and receives Jesus Christ as Saviour. The Holy Spirit responds by spiritually regenerating that individual and then taking up residence within him. As Teacher, Counsellor, Comforter, Enabler, and Intercessor, He embarks the believer on a one-way journey unto Christ-likeness.

A spiritual person will passionately aspire to holy living. Job viewed the matter of holiness as a crucial lifestyle: *"I made a covenant with mine eyes; why then should I think upon a maid" (Job 31:1)*? The Psalmist vowed, *"I will set no wicked thing before mine eyes" (Ps. 101:3).* Paul commands believers to *"abstain from all appearance of evil" (1 Thess. 5:22).* Holiness is not just not sinning; it is a mindset of being blameless, an attitude that loathes wickedness, and a heart that is determined to remain in the centre of God's will. Holiness demonstrates reverence for God.

Practically speaking, why might Paul be exhorting the older women to be reverent in behaviour? William MacDonald writes, "Deliver us from giddy women whose thoughts are centreed on frivolous matters!"[2] The application seems appropriate as it connects well in context to the next bit of exhortation—don't be slanderous.

Not False Accusers

The older women were not to be engaged in malicious gossip and slander. In fact, all believers should avoid these destructive habits, but perhaps Paul recognizes the propensity of these sisters to engage in such evil more readily than others. The Greek word *diabolos*, translated "devil" 34 times in the New Testament, is applied here. Literally, devil, when it is not a proper name, means "slanderer." Children of God are not to act like children of the devil. Paul emphatically teaches that a child of God should no longer walk *"according to the course of this world, according to the prince of the power of the air, the spirit that now worketh in the children of disobedience"* (Eph. 2:2).

Gossip is sin! Sometimes gossip manifests itself in the strangest formats, such as prayer requests and compliments. If you are not part of the problem or part of the solution in a matter, it is best not to get involved; just be still. Slander (*dibbah*) means "to defame or give an evil (unrighteous) report." Apparently, the older women were prone to jump to conclusions without all the facts, then deliberately and ungraciously share these presumptuous judgments with others. Such behaviour, at best, distorts the truth concerning the guilty and, at its worst, defames and defrauds the innocent. God is not glorified in either case.

> *There is he that speaketh like the piercings of a sword: but the tongue of the wise is health. —Proverbs 12:18*

> *A prudent man concealeth knowledge: but the heart of fools proclaimeth foolishness. —Proverbs 12:23*

> *In the multitude of words sin is not lacking, But he who restrains his lips is wise. —Proverbs 10:19 NKVJ*

Admiral Hyman Rickover of the U.S. Navy said, "Great minds discuss ideas. Average minds discuss events. Small minds discuss people."[3] The spiritual mind muses upon Christ and eternal truth. So reader, what kind of mind do you have? The tongue is the tail of the heart that wags out of the mouth for *"those things which proceed out of the mouth come forth from the heart; and they defile the man" (Matt. 15:18).*

Avoids Drunkenness

"And be not drunk with wine, wherein is excess; but be filled with the Spirit" (Eph. 5:18). Believers are not to be controlled or mastered by things or substances; they are to be controlled by the Holy Spirit. *"All things are lawful unto me, but all things are not expedient: all things are lawful for me, but I will not be brought under the power of any" (1 Cor. 6:12).* Why Paul exhorted the older women and not any other age/gender group concerning alcohol abuse is unclear; perhaps, being at home resulted in more opportunity, and if her children were married, a lesser degree of accountability would be present. Paul may have been warning those women enduring menopause not to resort to alcohol consumption to alleviate spells of depression and uneasiness associated with that time of life.

Teachers of Good Things

God instituted all human authority and responsibility. Whether social order (Gen. 9:6, Rom. 13:1-2), church order (Acts 14:23, 1 Tim. 3:1-13), or home order (Eph. 5:22-6:3, Col. 3:18-20), God has arranged every part of our existence so that we might learn submission to Him by yielding to the authority He has placed over us. Scripture strictly forbids women from engaging in the public teaching of the church when men are present (1 Cor. 14:33-34, 1 Tim. 2:11-12). Men symbolically represent God's glory (1 Cor. 11:7) and, thus, are to be the ones who speak for Him. So, what good things were the older women to teach? They were commissioned to teach younger women how to be better wives, mothers, and keepers of the home. Experience is a great teacher, and these older sisters had a wealth of practical knowledge in domestic affairs to pass down to the younger women. Such instruction would lessen the possibility of a new wife and mother needlessly repeating the past mistakes of others. Younger women should seek friendships with spiritually-minded older women; the result will expedite personal growth in accomplishing domestic responsibilities.

Sober (Minded)

A spiritual woman is one who is discrete and temperate—having control of her opinions and passions. The Greek word *sophronizo* is used here to speak of gaining a sound and disciplined mind. Discipline is not something we are born with—it must be learned. To hold one's tongue when your emotions are prompting you to ratify your position and declare your feelings requires discipline. To arise early from a good night's sleep to better serve the family and to accomplish the day's duties requires discipline. To submit to your husband's authority when you believe he is not acting in the best interests of the family requires tremendous self-control. This, however, is the behaviour of a sober-minded woman.

The disciplined woman is respectful to others, especially those in authority. Respectful communication is not an affront to submission; it is needed and welcomed by godly leaders. The sober minded-woman does not impose her personal preferences in a prominent or condescending way, nor is she confrontational unless holiness demands it. She relies on God's grace and wisdom and puts forth her best efforts to build up a godly home. *"Every wise woman buildeth her house: but the foolish plucketh it down with her hands" (Prov. 14:1).*

Affectionate to Her Husband

The Greek word *philandros* occurs only here in the New Testament; it means to "be fond of or affectionate to." A husband is commanded four times in Scripture to sacrificially love his wife, while the wife is to learn to be warm, kind and friendly towards her husband. Certainly, the husband is to be the initiator of love in the marriage relationship. As he loves his wife as Christ loves the Church, feelings of love will naturally well up within her. She will reciprocate these feelings back to her husband who initiated love, in the same way the Church naturally responds to Christ's love: *"We love Him, because He first loved us" (1 Jn. 4:19).*

Man was created to initiate and the woman to respond in the marriage relationship. Christ initiated love to gain a bride. It cost Him everything to reconcile sinners to Himself: first His glory, then His life. A lost sinner can reject the wooing plea of the Lord Jesus for salvation, but it is not wise to do so. Likewise, an affectionate wife does not withdraw from her husband's wooing nor does she withhold herself from satisfying his need for affection. She longs to be with her husband throughout the day and pays special attention to her personal appearance prior to his return. Above all, she seeks to be his intimate friend, helper, and life-long companion.

As she grows in Christ, she will seek to express love genuinely and frequently to her husband in the ways he most appreciates. Her love for him will be evident in both word and deed. She will respect her husband's authority in the home and, therefore, will make no major decisions without his approval. Her love is not critical or nagging and certainly does not contradict or demean him publicly. On the contrary, the affectionate wife is supportive and responsive.

A sister, who desires to remain anonymous, developed a study guide entitled *Be a Quality Woman.* In the lesson addressing Titus 2:4, she provides the following personal workout for wives:

Be Friends with Your Husband
Choose to be Friends!

Know your husband. (Gen. 2:24-25)
   List ten things you know are important to your husband.
   (If you can't list ten things, start talking and get to know him!)
   Plan to do (at least) one important thing for him a week.
Praise him everyday! (Prov. 19:13, 14).
   Make a list of (at least) five things you appreciate about him.
   Tell him today.
Stop criticizing him! I repeat, give the guy a break (Prov. 14:1)!
   What specific things make you crazy? Commit this to prayer!
   Plan activities to make him feel special.
 Put him first … before yourself, hobbies, girlfriends, children
      (Phil. 2:3).
   Name the things that you put before your husband. Now
      rearrange!
   Name (at least) five things he likes to do.
   Plan on sharing experiences together.
Obey God's commands for wives—shows love for God (John
   14:21).
   Help (Gen. 2:18).
   In which areas could you be helping your husband? Think!
Submit (Eph. 5:22).
   Is there an area presently in which you need to submit? Do it!
   Respect (Eph. 5:33).
   How do women demonstrate disrespect toward husbands?
   Do any of these things characterize you? Stop!
Pray for him! Begin a prayer journal for him including things like:
   List all the roles he plays in life.
   List the qualities God wants of him.
   List his projects.
   Every time you begin to nag, stop, and make it a request to God!

Affectionate to Her Children

Philoteknos, used only here in the New Testament; speaks of the maternal fondness a mother is to have for her children. It is related in behaviour to *philandros* (earlier mentioned in this verse) but has a different focus. One is marital affection, and the other is maternal tenderness. It seems strange that Paul would have to exhort young women to be friendly and kind towards their children, for the mother-child relationship is one of the strongest natural bonds. But there is a difference between providing for the temporal needs of a child and preparing them to serve the Lord. True maternal love includes teaching the Bible, an active prayer life, proper discipline, and encouragement. A spiritually-minded mother will be available to spend time with her children, to know them and to assist them in overcoming life's difficulties and their own character weaknesses. The excitement of going to a ballgame is temporary, but a child's appreciation and affection for parents who assist him or her in overcoming some emotional handicap or lingering impediment abides long afterwards.

Discreet

Sophron, translated "discreet" in verse 5 is the root form of *sophronizo,* which is translated as "sober" in verse 4. By applying the same word twice, Paul seems to be highlighting the characteristics of self-control, self-discipline, and prudence as being paramount traits of a godly woman.

Chaste

Chaste implies "clean" in the figurative sense. Scripturally speaking, it means "modest, pure, innocent, and clean." In view is sexual purity; it refers to faithfulness to one's husband, a clean thought life, wearing modest attire, and innocent responses. In the bedroom, a wife may wear or not wear whatever she desires, but in public, she should not seek to attract the attention of others, especially men. She should only desire to privately entice her husband. The chaste woman sees no value in reading romance novels or in watching inappropriate movies and soap operas. She is determined to maintain a pure, undefiled, and innocent thought-life. She is *"wise unto that which is good, and simple concerning evil" (Rom. 16:19).* Matthew Henry links the virtues of discretion and chastity together and then offers an urgent warning:

> *Discreet* and *chaste* stand well together; many expose themselves to fatal temptations by that which at first might be but indiscretion. *Discretion shall preserve thee, understanding shall keep thee from the evil way (Prov. 2:11). Chaste,* and *keepers at home,* are well joined too.[4]

Keepers at Home

"Keepers at home" doesn't mean she can never leave the home, but her desire and primary ministry is at home rather than elsewhere. As explained in an earlier chapter, the Greek meaning of *keeper at home* is "a guardian at home." Wives are to be gatekeepers; they are to keep out bad attitudes, elements that taint, and whatever might defile the household. They are to maintain an orderly home so that Satan does not establish a base of operation within (1 Tim. 5:14).

Prior to the addition of children to a family, a younger wife may find that she has the wherewithal to keep the home orderly and engage in some part-time employment. This family decision (to which the husband is held accountable) falls within the realm of liberty, but the home must not suffer. The reality of the matter is that a wife away from the home will be exposed to more evil, temptation and stress. The husband must spiritually evaluate the situation: "Is the extra money worth the cost?"

A young man who has his eye upon a prospective mate would do well to consider where she spends her time. Is her focus on domestic things, or is she preoccupied with matters and doings outside the home? A spiritually-minded woman will consider her home to be her refuge from the world, an abode where she can thrive and be protected. There is just no place like home!

Good

"Thou art good, and doest good" (Ps. 119:68). Goodness is an attribute of God, and all His doings are good. He is not selfish, but gracious and generous to others. A spiritual woman will be good to others. She will be given to hospitality, to assisting the needy, to encouraging the brokenhearted, and in general, she will live to serve others.

Obedient to Their Husbands

Obedient means "to submit to or be subject to." On this subject, Warren Wiersbe summarizes well God's plan for family order:

> God does all things *"decently and in order" (1 Cor. 14:40).* If He did not have a chain of command in society, we would have chaos. The fact that the woman is to submit to her husband does not suggest that the man is better than the woman. It only means that the man has the responsibility of headship and leadership in the home. Headship is not dictatorship or lordship. It is loving leadership. In fact, both the husband and the wife must be submitted to the *Lord* and to *each other* (Eph. 5:21). It is a mutual respect under the lordship of Jesus Christ.
>
> True spiritual submission is the secret of growth and fulfillment. When a Christian woman is submitted to the Lord and

to her own husband, she experiences a release and fulfillment that she can have in no other way. This mutual love and submission creates an atmosphere of growth in the home that enables both the husband and the wife to become all that God wants them to be. The fact that the Christian wife is "in the Lord" is not an excuse for selfish independence. Just the opposite is true, for her salvation makes it important that she obey the Word and submit to her husband.[5]

A young man considering a prospective bride should be observing whether she is willing to submit to the Lord. How does she submit to parental authority? Does she obey without complaining, or does she respond in an undermining way or with delayed obedience? Does she seem to second-guess her parents and make her own decisions? Like discipline, submission must be learned. Obedience can be forced, but submission is evidence of a yielded heart.

Summary

Perhaps, you have heard the old expression "pretty is as pretty does." It is true. Scripture emphasizes that *"women adorn themselves in modest apparel, with* [godly fear] *and sobriety; not with braided hair, or gold, or pearls, or costly array; but (which becometh women professing godliness) with good works" (1 Tim. 2:9-10).* Concerning wives, Peter states that it is *"the ornament of a meek and quiet spirit, which is in the sight of God of great price" (1 Pet. 3:4).* The outward appearance fades with age, but the inward beauty of a spiritually-minded woman is exquisite in the sight of God and appreciated by all that behold her life of "sound doctrine." Harriet Beecher Stowe once said, "So much has been said and sung of beautiful young girls, why doesn't somebody wake up to the beauty of old women?"[6] Might we all behold and appreciate the true beauty of godly women!

The Worth of a Virtuous Woman

Having a virtuous woman for a wife is a wonderful gift from the Lord. Solomon expressed the manifold blessings that a virtuous wife is to her husband:

He has obtained favour from the Lord (Prov. 18:22).

She is worth far more than rubies (Prov. 31:10).

She is not comparable to a great inheritance (Prov. 19:14)

She is a crown to her husband's head (Prov. 12:4).

King Solomon also highlighted the devastating influence a self-seeking and tumultuous woman may have upon her husband: *"A virtuous woman is a crown to her husband: but she that maketh* [him] *ashamed is as rottenness in his bones" (Prov. 12:4)*. A wife bent on discouraging her husband with harsh words, or worse, on hindering his spiritual growth Godward, is likened unto a cancer that rots his bones. Without healthy bones, we would be reduced to a pulsating blob of gushy tissue. Bones provide structure and stature to the body. How does one maintain healthy bones? Proverbs 15:30 states, *"A good report maketh the bones fat."* Truth, grace, honesty, encouragement, respect, and devotion all convey a "good report" to one's husband. *"Pleasant words are as an honeycomb, sweet to the soul, and health to the bones" (Prov. 16:24)*.

Scripture records many examples of wives who ministered to their husbands in such a way as to promote healthy stature and spiritual vitality; in doing so, each was a crown to her husband's head. Unfortunately, there are also biblical instances of women who influenced their husbands to flee higher reason, doubt God and to transgress His Word. Behaviour of this sort is likened to aggressive bone cancer. Instead of a "helpmeet," a wife of this kind becomes a "tripmate," and consequently, her husband's spiritual prominence wanes before God and man. Satan gains a victory in such cases, for God's creation order, which declares that the man represents God's glory on earth (1 Cor. 11:7), is unachieved. Consider the following examples of wives either being crowns to their husband's heads or being cancer to their bones:

A Crown to Her Husband's Head
1. *"Sarah obeyed Abraham, calling him lord"* (respected his authority, 1 Pet. 3:6).
2. *"Sarah conceived and bore Abraham a son"* (as God enabled, she gave Abraham children, Gen. 21:2 NKJV).
3. Rebekah covered herself with a veil to demonstrate respect to Isaac's authority (Gen. 24:65).
4. Rachel and Leah listened to Jacob and affirmed his leadership (Gen. 31:14-16).
5. Esther provided Ahasuerus with important information respectfully (Est. 2:22; 7:6).
6. The Proverbs 31 wife does her husband *"good and not evil all the days of her life" (Prov. 31:12).*
7. The Shulamite bride affirms her love to her groom the king (Song 1:13).
8. Priscilla co-laboured (often in their home) with her husband Aquila for the kingdom of God (Rom. 16:3-5; Acts 18:26).

Cancer to Her Husband's Bones

1. Eve was deceived and led Adam into sin (Gen. 3:6).
2. Sarah caused Abraham to doubt God's promise (Gen. 16:2).
3. Rebekah usurped Isaac's God-given authority in their home (Gen. 27:5-13).
4. Michal rebuked David for praising the Lord in dance (2 Sam. 6:20).
5. Job's wife instructed him to *"curse God and die" (Job 2:9).*
6. Solomon's many wives *"turned away his heart after other gods" (1 Kgs. 11:4).*
7. Jezebel stirred up Ahab *"to work wickedness in the sight of the Lord" (1 Kgs. 21:25).*
8. Athaliah caused Jehoram to walk *"in the way of the kings of Israel" (2 Chron. 21:6).*

Two general trends are observed in the above cases: (1) When the wife respected and submitted to her husband's authority (as unto the Lord), bore her husband children, helped her husband to serve God, spoke well of her husband, served her husband, and provided helpful information to her husband to assist his decision making, a good result was realized, and God's blessing was evident. (2) When the wife led her husband, caused her husband to doubt God's Word and working, rebuked her husband for his service to God, and stirred her husband up to lusting and idolatry, an evil result and consequence was realized.

Every wife has a choice concerning her husband's stature. She can be a cancer that rots his bones or a calcium supplement that promotes a strong skeletal structure. A wife choosing the latter will aid her husband in reaching his potential in the Lord through encouragement and accountability. Her principal thinking should be "he may not be the man he should be, but I will help him become the man he could be." Man gave up a bone to obtain woman; let the woman now endeavour to impart it back. The wife cannot take the place of the conviction and guidance of the Holy Spirit in her husband's life, but she can encourage him Godward and appreciate his notable labours of love to the family. This is an invaluable companionship and God's provision for man—for *"a prudent wife is from the Lord" (Prov. 19:14)*. Matthew Henry summarizes the special blessing that a prudent wife is to her husband:

> A discreet and virtuous wife is a choice gift of God's providence to a man—a wife that is *prudent,* in opposition to one that is contentious, (v.13). For, though a wife that is continually finding fault may think it is her wit and wisdom to be so, it is really her folly; *a prudent wife* is meek and quiet, and makes the best of every thing. If a man has such a wife, let him not ascribe it to the wisdom of his own choice or his own management (for the wisest have been deceived both in and by a woman), but let him ascribe it to the goodness of God, who made him a help meet for him."[1]

God created woman with a specific purpose in mind. God's general design for a woman (excluding those called to singleness) was to be a companion to her husband, to bear and nurture children and to keep an ordered home. As with every facet of our Christian experience, when we align our will with the will of God, we obtain immense joy and satisfaction in life. Only when a wife appreciates and apprehends true biblical femininity will she truly enjoy being a woman.

Unfortunately, many are not discovering God's simple message concerning womanhood. Ignorance of divine purpose and elevated human reasoning has only served to cause domestic misery. Sigmund Freud once reported, "Despite my thirty years of research into the feminine soul, I have not been able to answer ... the great question that has never been answered: what does a woman want?"[2] What a pity Mr. Freud did not consult the Bible for answers; he could have saved years of research.

We draw our study on biblical womanhood to a close by acknowledging one of many wives down through the corridors of time who have demonstrated the power of God through scriptural femininity. Her life serves as a memorial of God's grace and as a beacon of potential for every woman having the courage to yield herself to God's plan.

A Tribute to Emma Moody

D. L. Moody and Emma Revell married during the bloodiest era of American history. Their nation desperately needed to experience God's grace, and they felt they could better serve the Lord together for this cause. They shared a uniform passion for ministry which Emma clearly described, "Only the enterprises bearing eternal fruit, such as having a family and reaching lost souls, were important."[3] D. L. Moody was the energetic and gallant evangelist, while Emma was his trusted helper, encourager and voice of common sense. She sought her husband's welfare in all matters and co-laboured with him continuously. Shortly after their marriage, Emma wrote the following in her personal journal: "D. L. Moody and Emma C. Revell married on August 28, 1862. D. L. busy with *his* work among the soldiers."[4]

In her writings, her genuinely humble character is evident in that she did not mention her own vast ministry of serving union soldiers during the Civil War, including two lengthy trips to the front lines and ongoing work at Camp Douglas Chapel. Besides attending to the wounded and the distressed soldiers, she assisted the Sunday School mission and was busy visiting the poor, keeping the home in good order, and attending to guests, including D.L. Moody's chronically ill brother, Samuel.

In his book *The Life of D. L. Moody*, Lyle W. Dorsett highlights several particular ways in which Emma was a great blessing to her husband. The following are just a few.

Emma Moody did all she could to help her husband with the demanding schedule. She made clear that she would do all in her power to protect him from intruders who would take away the precious time he needed by himself and with God, so that he would have something worthwhile to give to his family and his public.[5]

The Moodys avoided the pitfalls that befell so many evangelists and missionaries because he and Emma made deliberate choices to be together. Making Northfield a home base ensured their having a place where the children always had relatives surrounding them. During the summers there were extended periods when the entire family including Mr. Moody, were together. They gathered for meals and family worship around their ornate Estey organ.[6]

It is true that D. L. Moody was frequently away from his family. Given the calling to itinerant work, however, he and Emma arranged family affairs as well as anyone could have. The secret of their family unity seems at core to reside in a keen sense of God's calling—his call on Mr. Moody to preach and His call on Mrs. Moody to serve God by supporting her husband and serving her children.[7]

Emma Moody no doubt helped keep D. L. alive longer by reminding him of priorities, saying no for him to others, and being his refuge when the pressures were strong and the opposition disconcerting. Emma Moody tended to many of the details, organization, and interpersonal issues that Dwight simply could not perform well.[8]

D. L. Moody died at home in Northfield, MA on December 22, 1899. While on his death bed, Mr. Moody turned his eyes to gaze upon his beloved Emma and softly uttered, "Mamma, you have been a good wife to me."[9] What more could be said; what more needed to be said? In one brief statement, D. L. Moody had summed up the life-long ministry of his wife. Emma had been superbly faithful! She was a reserved woman who never pursued fame or popularity but who sought only to please her Saviour by unselfish marital and maternal service. She has the praise of God, the praise of her husband, the praise of her children and the praise of millions of souls who were awakened to their spiritual need or stirred up in their Christian faith through the preaching of D. L. Moody. His sermons, writings, and the Bible Institute legacy in Chicago live on even to this day.

After Mr. Moody's home-calling, Emma continued to labour for the Lord, but her health declined abruptly after her husband's death. She died on October 10, 1903 at the age of sixty. Like D. L. Moody, Mrs. Moody finished well. The fact that all their children went on to impact the next generation for the Lord is an outstanding testimony of Emma Moody's maternal ministry. What is the worth of a virtuous woman?

End Notes

The First Marriage

1. Henry M. Morris, *The Genesis Record* (Baker Book House, Grand Rapids: 1976), p. 102
2. Matthew Henry, *Matthew Henry's Commentary* (MacDonald Publishing Co., McLean, VA: original 1706), Vol. 1, p. 20
3. Warren Wiersbe, *The Bible Exposition Commentary*, Vol. 2 (Victor Books, Wheaton, IL: 1989), p. 65
4. William Guest, *P. P. Bliss Songwriter* (Ambassador, Greenville, NC: 1997), p. 22

What is Headship?

1. G. Morrish, *A Concordance of the Septuagint* (Zondervan, Grand Rapids, MI: 1976), p. 136
2. "Headship," William Morris, *The American Heritage Dictionary* (Houghton Mifflin Company, Boston, MA: 1979)
3. William MacDonald, *Believer's Bible Commentary* (Thomas Nelson Publishers, Nashville, TN: 1995), p. 2084
4. J. Hunter, *What The Bible Teaches* (Ritchie, Scotland: 1982), pp. 124-125
5. J. Allen, *What The Bible Teaches* (Ritchie, Scotland: 1982), p. 207
6. K. Wuest, *Wuest's Word Studies* (Eerdmans, Grand Rapids, MI: 1978), Vol. 2, p. 48
7. C. H. Mackintosh, *Short Paper* (Believers Bookshelf, Sunbury, Vol. 2)

To Marry or Not?
1. William MacDonald, *The Disciple's Manual* (Gospel Folio Press, Port Colborne, ON: 2004), pp. 300-301
2. Warren Wiersbe, *The Bible Exposition Commentary*, op. cit., Vol. 1, p. 593
3. http://www.census.gov/acs
4. http://www.esa.un.org
5. Ibid.
6. http://www.usgovinfo.about.com/cs/censusstatictics
7. http://www.disastercentre.com/cdc.deathrate.html
8. Dr. Howard Taylor, *Spiritual Secret of Hudson Taylor* (Whitaker House, New Kensington, PA: 1996), p. 144
9. Gary Inrig, *Hearts Of Iron Feet Of Clay* (Chicago, IL: Moody Press: 1979), pp. 109-110
10. W. H. Bennet, *Robert C. Chapman of Barnstaple* (Pickering & Inglis, London: 1902), p. 127

Marital Satisfaction
1. H. Norman Wright, *The Premarital Counseling Handbook* (Moody Press, Chicago, IL: 1992), p. 157

The Perpetual Problem
1. David Augsburger, *When Caring is Not Enough* (Ventura, Calif. Regal Books: 1983), pp. 5-7
2. Warren Wiersbe, *The Bible Exposition Commentary*, op. cit., Vol. 2, p. 65

The Clinging Vine
1. Warren Wiersbe, *The Bible Exposition Commentary*, op. cit., Vol. 2, p. 230

Clusters of the Vine
1. C. E. Hocking, *Rise Up My Love* (Precious Seed Publication, West Glamorgan, UK: 1988), p. 54
2. Ibid., p. 187

Clusters of the Vine (cont.)

3. David Bercot, *A Dictionary of Early Christian Beliefs*—Veil (Hendrickson Publishers, Peabody, MA; 1998), p. 690
4. C. E. Hocking, op. cit., pp. 280-281
5. Warren Wiersbe, *Be Holy* (Victor books, Wheaton, IL: 1996), Lev. 15:1-33
6. Matthew Henry, op. cit., Vol. 3, p. 819

The Joyful Mother

1. 2002 Missionary Prayer Handbook (Christian Missions in Many Lands, Inc., Spring Lake, NJ; 2002)
2. Wendy Murray Zoba, *Women Reaching Women is Key in the Future of Missions* (*Christianity Today* August 7, 2000)
3. Edythe Draper, *Draper's Book of Quotations for the Christian World* (Tyndale House Publishers, Inc., Wheaton, IL), "Parents"

The Virtuous Woman

1. Matthew Henry, op. cit., Vol. 3, p. 975
2. John Phillips, *Exploring the Psalms*, (Kregel Academic & Professional, Grand Rapids, MI: 2002), Ps. 90:16
3. Sid S. Buzzell, "Proverbs," *The Bible Knowledge Commentary*. Ed. John F. Walvoord and Roy B. Zuck. (Victor Books, Wheaton, IL: 1985) p. 973

Building Her House

1. *Bless Your Heart* (Series 2) (Heartland Prairie, Inc, Eden Prairie, MN: 1990), 8.17

The Peaceful Home

1. William MacDonald, *My Heart, My Life, My All* (Gospel Folio Press, Grand Rapids, MI: 1997), p. 91
2. Edythe Draper, op. cit., "home"

The Widow
1. Warren Wiersbe, *Comforting the Bereaved* (Moody Press, Chicago, IL: 1985), p. 21
2. Ibid., p. 24

Ministry Opportunities
1. http://www.wisdomquotes.com

The Portrait of a Godly Woman
1. William MacDonald, *Believer's Bible Commentary*, op. cit., p. 2139
2. Ibid.
3. William MacDonald, *The Disciple's Manual*, op. cit., p. 290
4. Matthew Henry, op. cit., Vol. 6, p. 862
5. Warren Wiersbe, *The Bible Exposition Commentary,* op. cit., Vol. 2, p. 142
6. http://www.wisdomquotes.com

The Worth of a Virtuous Woman
1. Matthew Henry, op. cit., Vol. 3, p. 900
2. http://www.wisdomquotes.com
3. Lyle W. Dorsett, *The Life of D. L. Moody—A Passion for Souls* (Moody Press, Chicago, IL: 1997), p. 117
4. Ibid., 104
5. Ibid., 314
6. Ibid., 315
7. Ibid., 316
8. Ibid., 316
9. Ibid., 381

MIND FRAMES

The author shares six scriptural exercises to strengthen the mind's ability to focus Godward and then presents a dozen Christlike attitudes—mind frames—to guard our thoughts in challenging circumstances.

Binding: Paper   Page Count: 148
Category: Discipleship   ISBN: 1882701941

SEEDS OF DESTINY

This is a devotional book which explores Genesis in relation to the rest of Scripture. It contains over 100 devotions, and is suitable as either a daily devotional or as a reference source for deeper study.

Binding: Cloth   Page Count: 390
Category: Devotional   ISBN: 1897117019

YOUR HOME:
A BIRTHING PLACE FOR HEAVEN?

A practical guide to evangelism at home and in the workplace.

Binding: Paper   Page Count: 144
Category: Practical/   ISBN: 1882701739
Ministry

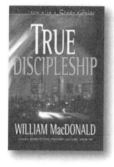
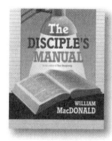

ON HIS HEART

A devotional which warms the heart and examines the wonderful ways of the Lord at work.

Binding: Paper   Page Count: 168
Category: Devotional   ISBN: 1882701593

AT HIS FEET

Where would you go when your spirit longed to know God? To His Feet of course. The feet where Mary sat, the feet that where nailed to a cross. Where every knee shall bow.

Binding: paper   Page Count: 198
Category: Devotional   ISBN: 1882701062

IN HIS HANDS

A devotional book which focuses on placing trust in God. The author shares personal experiences that call our hearts to trust God.

Binding: Paper   Page Count: 160
Category: Devotional   ISBN: 1882701275

AT HIS TABLE

It is a privilege to feast at His table & share His blessed hope with others at our tables, & what a joy it will be to feast in the presence of the Lord when He returns.

Binding: paper   Page Count: 144
Category: Devotional   ISBN: 1882701984

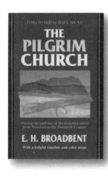

THE PILGRIM CHURCH
BY E. H. BROADBENT

This book examines often ignored church history. It outlines courageous people who chose to follow Christ. This engaging book will thrill your heart with stories of heroes of the faith, and will spur you on to greater devotion to the Lord and to a deeper concern for His suffering people around the world.

Binding: Cloth
Category: Church History

Page Count: 468
ISBN: 1882701534

HOLY GROUND:
53 MEDITATIONS ON ISAIAH 53
COMPLIED BY BRIAN GUNNING

The most precious time of all Christian gatherings is the Lord's Supper. This book has been prepared with this in mind—a collection of meditations on the beloved Isaiah 53.

Binding: Bonded Leather
Category: Devotional

Page Count: 232
ISBN: 1897117027

ACCORDING TO LUKE
BY DR. DAVID GOODING

In this fresh and original approach to the Gospel of Luke, David Gooding uses a careful analysis of the Gospel's literary structure to bring out Luke's unique presentation of the person and work of Christ.

Binding: paper
Category: Expository

Page Count: 362
ISBN: 1882701801